FIRST IN TRINIDAD
BY MICHAEL ANTHONY

Paria Classics

FIRST IN TRINIDAD

BY MICHAEL ANTHONY

PARIA PUBLISHING COMPANY

Published by
Paria Publishing Company Limited
Second Avenue, Cascade, Trinidad, W.I.
Email: paria@trinidad.net

OTHER PARIA PUBLICATIONS BY THE SAME AUTHOR:

The Making of Port-of-Spain Vol. 1 (1757 - 1939)
The Making of Port-of-Spain Vol. 2 (1939 - 1945)

Printed by Lightning Source, U.S.A.

ISBN 976-8054-51-4

DEDICATION
To Jennifer, Keith, Carlos, Sandra,
and of course, to Yvette.

CONTENTS

PUBLISHERS' NOTE

Michael Anthony was one of the first authors to be published by
Paria Publishing Company in the 1980s, and his superbly researched,
informative and entertaining books have found their way into public
and private libraries, the Trinidad and Tobago educational system,
and many other institutions at home and abroad.

We are proud to re-introduce several of his works, many of which
have been long out-of-print, to the history lover and researcher.
Especially for young readers, Michael Anthony as a writer combines
the rare ability to bring across historical facts in a way that makes you
feel as though you just read a short story, not a scholarly text.

We congratulate him on his honorary doctorate, awarded by the
University of the West Indies in 2003, and we are happy that "First In
Trinidad" also marks the first publication in our Paria Classics series,
a programme in which we will re-publish the out-of-print titles of some
of our country's best historians.

It is perhaps not a coincidence that we commence the Paria
Classics series in the same year that the National Library of Trinidad
and Tobago opened its doors to the public, indeed a joyous occasion
that we would like to mark with this publication.

Please enjoy "First in Trinidad"!

Gerard Besson
Trinidad, September 2003

AUTHOR'S NOTE

This book tells of the very first occasions that certain significant events took place in Trinidad.

In a few cases, the events themselves did not take place in Trinidad, but concern Trinidad. An example of this is the account, "The First World Champion", which centres on Claude Noel's boxing victory in Atlantic City, United States, in 1981; or "The First Olympic Champion", which is the story of Hasley Crawford's success at the Montreal Olympics of 1976.

Although this historical survey relates almost entirely to Trinidad, there are four episodes in respect to Tobago. These are: "The Name Tobago", "The First Attempt at Settlement", "The First Permanent Settlement" and "The First House of Assembly".

And, of course, there are studies that feature both islands, such as the stories of the General Elections of 1925 and 1946, and "The frst time we could say 'Trinidad and Tobago', which is the story of the political linking of the two islands.

In all, the book contains 55 episodes. Apart from those already mentioned, it deals with such subjects as the first town in Trinidad, the first police force, the first newspapers, the first Carnival of the streets, the first time ice came, the first primary schools, the first postal service, the coming of electricity, the coming of the telephone, the first tram, the first trains, and the first buses.

There is also a description of the first time the steelbands came out onto the streets.

It is hoped that "First in Trinidad" will lend an insight into some of the historic junctures of our past.

Michael Anthony
St. James, 2003

*A*CKNOWLEDGEMENTS

Thanks are due for the help and kind courtesies extended to the author by the staff of the National Archives and the Reference Libraries in Port-of-Spain—especially the reference section of the Trinidad Public Library.

Thanks are also due to Christine Tavani for proof-reading the manuscript.

CHAPTER ONE

THE FIRST TIME THIS ISLAND WAS CALLED TRINIDAD (1498)

The first time this island was called "Trinidad" was on that far-off Tuesday, at noon, when Christóbal Colon and the people sailing with him spotted its southern hills.

The date was 31 July, 1498, and Christóbal Colon, who was sailing for Spain, was on his third voyage of discovery.

Christóbal Colon, known to the English-speaking world as Christopher Columbus, would never have come upon this island had he not radically departed from the course of his two former voyages.

He had left the port of San Lucar, in Southern Spain, on 30 May, 1498, and after heading for Madeira and then the Canary Islands, he set his course more southerly than he had done before, hoping to find the mysterious "Dom João Land" that was said to be on the equator. As he steered to the southwards (while moving westerly), the heat was so great that he became very concerned. Also, the wind was not at all favourable. He wrote: "The wind then failed me, and I entered a climate where the intensity of the heat was such that I thought both ships and men would burn up, and everything suddenly got into such a state of confusion, that no man dared go below deck to attend to the securing of the water-casks and the provisions."

This heat lasted eight days, at the end of which it happened that he got a favourable wind, and he decided that because of the temperature he would abandon the south-western course and head due west. At this point, he was anxious for any sign of land, for he wanted to repair the vessels as well as take in water and renew the stock of provisions. And he was probably beginning to think of Haiti, too, the island he had called "Hispaniola," where he had established a settlement on his second voyage. He had already turned northward when the crucial moment came.

When Columbus had been preparing to set out from San Lucar, he had made a vow to heaven that the first land he discovered he would name after the Blessed Trinity. It is important to say this now, but let us go back to Columbus and the moment of his great discovery. Columbus wrote in his log: "At the end of seventeen days, during which the Lord granted me a favourable wind, on Tuesday 31 July, at noon, land presented itself to our gaze. ... And as the Lord High has always shown mercy to me, one of the sailors, happening to climb to the maintop, saw a range of three mountains to the westward ... I then abandoned the northward course and turned towards the land."

There was of course great joy on board, for everyone had begun to feel afraid that the admiral would not reach land. They sang the "Salve Regina" and gave thanks to God. Columbus remembered his vow to name the first land he saw after the Blessed Trinity—the three persons in One God, according to the Roman Catholic faith. The word "Trinity" in Spanish is *la trinidad*, and so Columbus cried out "La Trinidad!", claiming the island for Spain.

Columbus approached the land and he said he reached a cape which he called "Cape Galea", a place that is today known as Point Galeota. Here, there was a harbour, but no good anchorage.

THE FIRST ENCOUNTER OF THE
AMERINDIANS WITH THE SPANISH
SAILORS

Columbus added: "Here are houses and people and very fair lands, lands as beautiful and green as the gardens of Valencia in the month of March."

These are Columbus' very words, but it is very unlikely that he could have seen houses and people there. However, it is the naming of the island that interests us now. This island was called by its natives, Kairi, meaning, "the island close to the mainland". On Tuesday, 31 July, in the year 1498, Christopher Columbus named it: *Trinidad*.

THE FIRST INHABITANTS OF WHAT
WAS TO BE NAMED "TRINIDAD"
WERE MIGRANTS FROM THE SOUTH
AMERICAN MAINLAND.

CHAPTER TWO

THE FIRST OUTSIDERS TO SET FOOT IN TRINIDAD (1531)

A lthough in 1498, some of Columbus' sailors, in coming ashore to get water, would have been the first "outsiders" to touch Trinidad soil, we can omit this brief incident and consider the occasion when the first intruders, or invaders, came to this country.

For this, we have to turn to the year 1531, when a man appointed governor of Trinidad by the Crown of Spain arrived here to take up office. He could not come in the way a governor is expected to come and take office. In 1531, Trinidad was completely Arawak, and despite the fact that Christopher Columbus had claimed possession of the island for Spain, nothing had happened since 1498, and the Arawak peace was complete and undisturbed.

The man appointed governor of Trinidad was Antonio Sedeño, who was at the time a Spanish official from the island of Puerto Rico. Apparently, Sedeño, who desired to be a conquistador, wrote to the Spanish court saying that he had "pacified" the Arawak island of Trinidad, and he asked to be made governor. This claim was of course far from the truth. The King of Spain replied: "Inasmuch as you, Antonio Sedeño, our Contador of the Island of San Juan, Puerto Rico, zealous for the service of the Kingdom of God, and of our Realms, have offered to construct a fort in the Island of Trinidad and to establish a priest there to baptise the Indians, and that you will do all that is

5

necessary to settle the said island and to encourage the Indians there to accept our Holy Roman Catholic faith, in consequence of which we have approved an agreement with you ... We promise and do now hereby appoint you to be our Governor of this said island for all the days of your life, provided that for the Governorship you receive no salary whatsoever, until such time that we do order that a *residencia* be taken to assess your Governorship." (A *residencia* was usually two or three people sent out from Spain and forming a court in a place where a governor was resident, to listen to complaints against him by the citizens. This was done as a means of assessing his performance.)

In that same year, 1531, Sedeño arrived here with a force of 80 men, and tried to effect a landing. He had entered the Gulf of Paria through the Serpent's Mouth, using the route Columbus had taken, and he had apparently made friends with a peaceful cacique in the south. Maybe it was at the instigation of this cacique that he headed north, sailing right up the Gulf of Paria.

The warlike Arawak tribes of the north heard of Sedeño's progress and massed to repulse him. Sedeño steered straight for the Arawak village of Cu-Mucurapo and landed in the face of a shower of bows and arrows. Sedeño unleashed his superior fire-power against the Arawaks and the hostile forces fought all day. Both sides suffered heavily. During the battle, the Arawaks lost their cacique and retreated, but they returned the next day and fought bitterly until sunset, giving no quarter. Although many more Arawaks than Spaniards fell in the battle, the Spaniards had begun with only 80 men and the Arawaks had thousands. At one point of the battle, Sedeño found that he had lost 50 men, and now he was forced to withdraw across the Gulf to the Spanish Main to seek help.

When Sedeño and his men returned to Trinidad, the Arawaks pretended to be offering peace, appearing to welcome the Spaniards warmly, but once the Spaniards were on shore, the Arawaks turned on them suddenly, killing 21. Sedeño himself had to flee. Hastening on board, he escaped by cutting the cables of his ship.

Yet, the Spanish conquistador returned. He came back with an ample force and revenge in his heart, and this time he routed the enemy in a night attack. They continued to bear down on him from all sides and he could not settle, and in the end they reduced his numbers so critically that he was forced to go back again. The proud and tenacious Sedeño, however, came yet another time in an attempt to crush Arawak resistance, for was he not governor of Trinidad? He came with all manner of reinforcements, and this time something happened. Something dramatic and totally unexpected. Among Sedeño's reinforcements were monster beasts, beasts never before seen in these parts. What creatures were they? Horses! On seeing mounted horsemen the Arawaks broke ranks and ran. Believing man and beast were one, they fled in panic. With this sudden victory, Sedeño's battle was over.

But no sooner had Sedeño gained this victory that there was the cry of gold in Peru. Francisco Pizzaro had captured the rich Inca treasures in Peru. Trinidad had no gold, and Sedeño's men did not see why they should have to face Arawak arrows in vain. The cry was Peru! Most of Sedeño's men deserted him, and afterwards he was betrayed to a rival conquistador who was seeking to establish a settlement on the mainland across the Gulf. In the end Sedeño was captured, taken across the Gulf and imprisoned, and he later died broken-hearted.

It was a sad end to this bold and impetuous man who in 1531 led the first of the "outsiders" to set foot in Trinidad.

DON ANTONIO SEDEÑO,
FIRST SPANISH GOVERNOR OF
TRINIDAD (1530-1538)

CHAPTER THREE

THE FIRST TOWN IN TRINIDAD (1592)

T he site of the first town to be established in Trinidad came into existence on 15 May, 1592—the day that a conquistador forced his way up the Caroni and took possession of a piece of land a few miles up the river. The conquistador was Domingo de Vera, *maestro de campo* of new governor of Trinidad, Antonio de Berrio.

Antonio de Berrio had left Spain in 1580 with a royal commission to find the golden land, believed to have been somewhere in the vicinity of today's Guyana. De Berrio wasted no time. By 1590 he had already made two unsuccessful attempts to find El Dorado, but obsessed with the desire for the fortune and fame that discovery would bring, he decided to make a third attempt. He had been named governor of Margarita, an island just off the north coast of the Spanish Main, but this did not satisfy him, as he felt he would like to be a little nearer to the field of his search. It was as a result of this, following a petition to the King of Spain, that he was appointed governor of the Arawak island of Trinidad.

De Berrio sent Domingo de Vera to conquer the island and establish a settlement. Fortunately for de Vera, Antonio Sedeño, the conquistador, had alread spread fear in the native peoples by his merciless campaign of some decades before, during which he must have slaughtered thousands of Arawaks. Although Sedeño had not settled, the Arawaks of Trinidad could not have wanted to engage the Spaniards in battle anymore. However, Domingo arrived at the island, and after putting in at a place of silk cotton trees, called Cu-Mucurapo, and treating with some caciques there, he decided to sail up the Caroni. Somewhere toward its headwaters he and his soldiers alighted, and being then given land to settle upon by the cacique Goangoanare, de Vera took possession of the place in the name of Spain and of his master, Antonio de Berrio.

De Vera did this in colourful fashion, calling on his soldiers to witness the scene. He pointed out that the place was bounded on the east by a high hill, on the south by a *vega* or flat bank, on the west by rolling, hilly land, and on the north by a mountain pass. Crying out that he would defend the spot with his life for the King of Spain and for Antonio de Berrio, he drew his sword and issued a challenge to anyone who would take the land from him. The soldiers, in response, shouted "Viva el Rey!" and de Vera proceeded to mark out the sites of four buildings around a huge central square.

The four buildings, basic requirements for the establishment of any Spanish town, were the Casa Real or Government House, a Cabildo or Town Hall, a church and a prison. He christened the place San José de Oruña—the town we know as St. Joseph today.

Antonio de Berrio arrived here later in the year and took up residence at San José de Oruña, thus confirming it as the capital of Trinidad. As governor he hardly governed, and in any case there was hardly anything to govern. He turned to his chief purpose of coming to Trinidad: organising an expedition to El Dorado. He had his *maestro de campo* along with him, his aging general, Alvaro Jorge, and the rest of the citizens of San José de Oruña was a complement of about 70 soldiers.

De Berrio came here only to mount an expedition to El Dorado, and if this point was in danger of being forgotten, then de Berrio's letter of New Year's Day 1593 should remind of it. Addressed to the King of Spain, de Berrio declares: "I went to Trinidad as it was of importance to me to see and examine it ... I found that it was thickly populated with natives ... It is a very good country for ginger, but the best thing about it is its nearness to the Main."

It was the quest for El Dorado that led to the settlement of Trinidad, and of course the establishment of its first town. And we look back to the historic date, 15 May, 1592, when a piece of land at the headwaters of the Caroni River became San José de Oruña, Trinidad's first town.

CHAPTER FOUR

THE FIRST CHURCH (1592)

THE FIRST CHURCH (1592)

The first Roman Catholic church in Trinidad was built at St. Joseph, which, as San José de Oruña, was the first town established in Trinidad. San José de Oruña was founded by Domingo de Vera in 1592, and Domingo, blazing a trail for Antonio de Berrio who was soon to arrive here as Governor, marked out the site of a church.

This church was among the first four buildings to be constructed in Trinidad, the others marked out on the same occasion were a *Casa Real* or Government House, a Cabildo, and a prison. These four buildings were to have been constructed around a square, the typical layout for a Spanish town.

The date that Domingo de Vera arrived at San José, received the land from the Amerindians, and marked out the site for the church and other buildings was the 15 May, 1592. Governor Antonio de Berrio did not arrive to take up his appointment until the end of that year.

Not much is known of that church except that it could not have been as magnificent a structure as the houses of worship in Spain. Everything points to the fact that it could have been nothing but a makeshift wooden structure, thatched with either carat or tirite leaves. Also, it could not have lasted more than three years, for we know that when Sir Walter Raleigh came to Trinidad in 1595, he marched on San José, captured Antonio de Berrio, sacked the town, and burned it to the ground. This church, which had been called San

View of St. Joseph by Michel-Jean Cazabon

Antonio de Padua by Governor de Berrio (after the 12th-century priest), disappeared without trace. Governor Antonio de Berrio died in 1597, and his son Fernando, who succeeded him, must have placed the reconstruction of the church as among the most urgent tasks in his rebuilding of the town. He built it on the same site. It is not certain what happened in between, but in 1649, San José was again sacked and burnt—this time in a Dutch raid from Tobago, as a reprisal against the then governor, Martin Mendoza. The church was rebuilt of thatch and tapia, and again on the same site.

Nothing appears to have stirred the chroniclers until fifty years later, when there came another big event in the annals of that church. It was a grave and terrible event—an event that has been called "The Arena Massacre". During a period of tension between the Amerindians and the Spaniards at Arena, the Amerindians of the Mission of San Francisco de los Arenales waylaid the Governor, who was going to Arena on a visit, and they killed him and other members of his party as well as Catholic priests of the mission itself. Spanish troops retaliated and killed hundreds of Amerindians in revenge. The dead bodies of the priests were transported from the Mission of Arena—which was near the site that the village of San Rafael occupies today—and taken to the Catholic church of San José for burial. Beneath the floor of the church a hole was dug and the bodies were laid to rest.

We know that at that point the church was on the same site, for two reasons. One of the reasons is the following: there is, even today, a gravestone in the yard of that church that carries the date 1682 —17 years before the massacre, so the church could not have been moved. The other reason we shall see shortly.

When the British captured Trinidad in 1797, Chacón, during the turbulence, had fled to San José, and the ceremony of surrender took place in the square in front of that church.

The structure was not to last too long afterwards, for Woodford, in the early British days, was besieged with pleas for the rebuilding of the Anglican church in Port-of-Spain—a church destroyed in the fire of 1808. Of course, at that stage, Port-of-Spain had long become the capital of Trinidad.

While Governor Woodford was seeking funds to rebuild the Anglican church, and while the Catholics of Port-of-Spain were themselves calling for a new Catholic church, the proud Catholics of San José donated money and started building a new Catholic church— the impressive structure that stands today. It did receive a good deal of government help, for a letter from Woodford to the Secretary of State for the Colonies, Earl Bathurst, of 8 February, 1816, says: "A new church has been lately commenced at St. Joseph to which I granted 2,000 pounds last year from the Colonial Treasury and which I am now called upon to extend in a similar amount, that the building may be completed..." Up to that time, the only other Catholic church in Trinidad was the delapidated Catholic church in Tamarind Square, Port-of-Spain.

This San José church rallied as it was until 1966, when some restoration work was carried out. In tiling the floor the ground beneath was interfered with, apparently for the first time since 1699. The result was that many human bones were brought to the surface. So this is the second reason why we know that the church remained on its original site. Therefore, in looking at the Catholic church of St. Joseph we are looking at the spot where, centuries before, Domingo de Vera and his men marked out the site of what was to become the first house of worship in Trinidad.

CHAPTER FIVE

THE NAME TOBAGO

obago, together with Barbados, has the distinction of not having been discovered by Christopher Columbus—one of the only two inhabited islands in these parts to have escaped the attention of the great explorer.

And who were these people, the earliest inhabitants? The Caribs, of course, so far as history states. The Caribs were a group of people who as a rule moved from place to place in search of food. They are reputed to have come from the Guianas in South America, and to have moved up the islands, leaving in their wake a path of blood and terror. Unlike the Arawaks, who inhabited Trinidad and the bigger islands of the West Indies, the Caribs were not eaters of meal and fish, but eaters of flesh—human flesh! In fact, "Carib" was the word Columbus heard when on his first voyage of discovery in 1492, he was told about these people by the inhabitants of Haiti. He was also told they came from a province called *Caniba*, hence the word "cannibal".

However, the Caribs, who have been said to have overrun the smaller islands and to have moved on when the human food was no more, seemed to have stayed in Tobago and to have settled to some extent. They did not only stay and settle but became well-known for trade. They planted a crop known for its aromatic leaves, when dried, and which, it appeared, they bartered with other native peoples of the region.

For the native peoples were fond of burning the leaves of this plant and inhaling the smoke and savouring of the aroma, through what they called a *tobaco*, now called a pipe. The crop was grown extensively on this island, the island came to be called by the name of the pipe.

The Courlanders and Dutch, who first settled the island, knew it by its Carib name of Tobaco, which soon became corrupted to Tobago, with the "ba" pronounced "bar" as in tobacco. The English, who came along in the mid-eighteenth century, gave it the pronounciation that we have today: *Tobaygo*.

THE FIRST TIME THAT EUROPEANS
SAW THE CARIBS SMOKING WAS OUT
OF A TUBE CALLED A "TABACO" A
HERB KNOWN AS "COHIBA".

CHAPTER *SIX*

THE FIRST ATTEMPT TO SETTLE TOBAGO (1625)

T obago, one of the only two islands in this region Christopher Columbus did not "discover", came into recorded history only in 1625, when the first attempt was made to settle it.

Before that it was not entirely unknown, for we know that a group of English sailors visited this island in 1580. They did not stay, but they left the Union Jack tied to a tree—meaning that they had claimed the island for England.

The people who tried to settle Tobago in 1625 were British settlers from Barbados. In a way, it is coincidental that they should have come from Barbados, because Barbados was the other island that Columbus did not encounter. However, the new settlers arrived in Tobago to a reception that could have only been described as terrifying. At that stage, the Caribs were masters of Tobago and they had no intention of welcoming intruders.

The group seeking to settle was led by the Reverend Nicholas Leverton, who, with his followers, felt that they could not accept what they described as the sinful life being led in Barbados.

But the experience on arriving at Tobago must have been far more bewildering. As soon as the group came ashore they met such a hostile assault by the Caribs that they had to flee for their lives. Most of them fell to the Carib arrows, and the few that escaped, did so by swimming back to their boats. Reverend Leverton himself barely escaped. He had sustained a head wound and must have swum in a dazed condition. In any case, what with the Caribs being such good boatmen, the rest of the group was lucky to arrive back in Barbados alive. Like all stubborn settlers, they had lived to fight another day.

From that date, things were never to be the same again. The Caribs felt suspicious and uneasy, and their fears were completely justified, for they were never left in peace from that time onward.

Three nations in particular became obsessed with settling Tobago: the English, the French, and the Dutch. Indeed, because of those seamen of 1580, the English felt that Tobago belonged to them. So much was this so that the very year after Leverton's attempt—1626—the English King, Charles I, gave a charter to the Dutch West India Company to establish a settlement in Tobago. As a result of obtaining the charter, the Dutch sent a party to settle in 1628, but again the Caribs wreaked havoc on them, driving them out. Five years later the Dutch tried again, and this time they succeeded in establishing a settlement, which they called Nieuw Walcheren. This is where Charlotteville is now. Oddly enough, the Caribs did not seem to attack the settlement of Nieuw Walcheren, but the Spaniards of Trinidad did not feel very comfortable having the Dutch so near to them, and they sent an expedition in the night and scared the Dutch away.

The English, confident of their ownership of Tobago, brought the Courlanders into the picture when in 1641 Charles I gave Tobago as a birthday present to his godson, James, Duke of Courland (Courlandia was the little duchy that later became Latvia). The Duke promptly sent settlers to Tobago in 1642. Although this attempt at settlement also failed because of the Caribs, one of its effects was to get a united attempt of the English, French and Dutch to crush Carib resistance in Tobago. As a result, when the second batch of Courlanders arrived in Tobago in 1654, what remained of the Caribs could do nothing to oppose the settlers. Six hundred men, women, and children arrived on that occasion. They came ashore in what is now Courland Bay, and they established the first permanent settlement in Tobago.

CHAPTER SEVEN

THE FIRST PERMANENT SETTLEMENT IN TOBAGO (1763)

W hen in 1654 six hundred men, women, and children from Courland landed in what came to be called Great Courland Bay, and proceeded to establish a settlement, two Dutchmen that same year sent a number of people from Holland to settle on the opposite side of the island.

The Courlanders were sent by James, Duke of Courland, to whom the English King, Charles I, had earlier given Tobago, and the Dutch were sent by the brothers Adrian and Cornelius Lampsins, because Holland, too, felt she had a right to Tobago. The very Charles I, who had presented Tobago to the Duke of Courland in 1642, had in 1626 granted a charter to the Dutch West India Company to establish a settlement in the island.

The two groups—the Courlanders and the Dutch—lived side by side, the first on the shores of Great Courland Bay, and the second on the shores of what we now know as Rockly Bay (Roquely Bay). They had no enemies within the island because the Caribs were already bludgeoned into subjection. The only possible hostility could have arisen between themselves, but since Holland and Courland were at the time bound by a treaty of friendship, a very cordial relationship existed between the two. However, drama came in 1658, for on the scenario of European rivalry, Courland fell to the Swedes, and the Duke of Courland was imprisoned. In Tobago, instead of showing sympathy to the Courlanders, the Dutch marched over and seized the Courlanders' territory, bringing it under Dutch rule.

While the Dutch felt secure in their dominion over Tobago, the British had not surrendered their claim, and indeed the picture was to become more complicated, when the French were staking a claim. The French declared that in 1656 a Frenchman, who had been shipwrecked on Tobago, had claimed the island for France. Based on this claim Louis XIV of France made Tobago available to the Dutch West India Company.

On the other hand, the British, who had taken note of the Dutch seizure of the Courlanders' territory in 1658, now called on the Dutch to withdraw. The Dutch refused and an English expedition sailed on Tobago and captured it.

Then the French came into the picture for the first time, and in the most curious way. The British had left a garrison of fifty men at Great Courland Bay, and shortly after the rest had departed, 25 men from the French garrison at Grenada landed unobserved in Courland Bay. On landing they made such an awful racket with their drums that the English believed that the enemy consisted of a great number of men, and that what they were seeing were only the advance guard. This was exactly what the French had intended. The French commander called on the British to surrender, saying that he did not want to spill unnecessary blood, and that the entire French force was just down the hill. The British gave up their arms and the 25 Frenchmen took over the fort.

The Frenchmen were really soldiers of fortune and had no interest in Tobago. The commander, Monsieur Vincent, kept a garrison there until March 1667. Then he set fire to everything and he and his men withdrew.

The Dutch then seized the opportunity to re-occupy Tobago. They returned to where they had been before, on the shores of Rockly Bay, which name they now changed to Lampsins Bay. They made a street, built houses, a church, and wharves. They built an impressive star-shaped fort, with the governor's house in the middle of it, and in it also

17TH CENTURY DUTCH SETTLERS. INSET: BARON LAMPSINS, WHO WAS ONE OF THE FIRST GOVERNORS OF TOBAGO.

was an arsenal of ammunition and gun-powder. They called the town Lampsinsburg.

This beautiful and compact little town of Lampsinsburg was the scene of one of the bloodiest battles in Tobago's history. In 1677, during a war between France and Holland, 1,000 Frenchmen made an assault on Lampsins Bay, and in a bitter engagement with the Dutch a French ball dropped in the gunpowder magazine of the fort. The explosion which followed was so severe it seemed to rock the whole island. The Dutch commander and about 250 of his men were blown to bits.

The French could have easily taken Tobago then, but they did not want it. In any case, their possession of Tobago would not have lasted long, for the Treaty of Nimeguen in 1679 restored Tobago to the Dutch.

After many such encounters, and many, many more years, what looked like peace finally came to Tobago. England captured Tobago from France in 1762, and in 1763 the British declared Tobago a self-governing and independent state. Settlers poured in from Barbados and a great number also came from England. Lampsinsburg was enlarged, and the English changed the name to Scarborough. More drama was in the offing, for example, Tobago was to fall three more times before it finally remained British. This settlement was the first permanent settlement in Tobago.

THE TOBAGO HOUSE OF ASSEMBLY

CHAPTER EIGHT

THE FIRST HOUSE OF ASSEMBLY (1768)

F ollowing a period of unquiet in Tobago, from the time it was first settled by Europeans in 1628, up to the British campaign of 1762 (during which it changed hands more than a dozen times), a period of peace seemed in the offing, and this could be seen by the number of settlers now crowding into Tobago.

The British in this period seemed to have had a strong navy, and when in 1762 they wrested Tobago from the French, a great number of settlers, mainly from Barbados, chose to make Tobago their home. This was especially so after the Treaty of Paris of 1763 confirmed Tobago as British.

The new British settlers founded a town not too far from the old Dutch settlement of Lampsinsburg, which was first established more than 100 years before. Tobago had changed hands several times since then, but the site of Lampsinsburg, once made into a near impregnable fort by the Dutch, had always attracted newcomers. Some of the new British settlers had come here too, but the majority founded the settlement nearby, which they named Georgetown, in honour of the then English king, George III.

In October 1763, Tobago was declared an independent, self-governing territory, and a General Council was appointed to administer it. Eleven planters formed this council.

Shortly before this General Council was appointed, Governor Robert Melville, who was head of the Grenada Government (which now included Tobago) sent Alexander Brown to Tobago to govern the island. Brown had the authority to establish a House of Assembly when he thought fit, depending on the situation in the island. Lieutenant-Governor Alexander Brown arrived in the island in November 1764, at a time when the island had just been divided into parishes and a great deal of land was sold. Melville, who was in overall charge, must have been very serious about the development of Tobago, for he decreed that in every parish land had to be provided for the setting up of a town. This was not practicable. However, the development of Tobago continued at so fast a rate that the Legislative Council and Assembly held their first session in the capital, Georgetown, on 16 April, 1768.

On that occasion the Legislators enacted five laws, and this episode is in itself memorable because the Crown showed its power by disallowing all five of those laws, deeming them to be objectionable.

Georgetown might have been chosen as the first capital by these British settlers from Barbados—who, incidentally, called its bay Barbados Bay—but it was Lampsinsburg, the former Dutch town, that seemed the more desirable place. At least the settlers at Georgetown felt so, because they drifted to Lampsinsburg in great numbers. They decided that the Dutch name was no longer good enough for them. Many of them must have originally come from Yorkshire, and must have thought they saw a resemblance between Lampsinsburg and the English seaside town of Scarborough, for Scarborough was the name they now gave to the place. In fact, on a map as early as 1765 it bears the name Scarborough, and this must have been the first time it appeared in this way. Georgetown did not survive long as the capital of Tobago. The House of Assembly at Georgetown, which had seen the first Legislative Council sitting in April 1768, was transferred to Scarborough in 1769, thereby making Scarborough the capital of Tobago.

The members of this House of Assembly took many positive steps. Between the years 1777 and 1799 it ordered the building of Fort King

VIEW OF SCARBOROUGH
BY CAPTAIN WILSON (1847)

George, on the hill above the town, to protect Scarborough in case of attack. Measures for the functioning and management of Tobago brought in a new day, and this coincided with an upsurge in the production of the main crops: sugar, rum, indigo, and cotton.

Scarborough, which at the time of the British capture in 1762 was deserted except for a few people and the silent French fort, now had a bustling population of about 3,000 people.

The present building used as a House of Assembly was started in 1821 and completed in 1825, during the administration of Governor F.P. Robinson. The building was originally constructed as a Court House and Public Office, but on its completion it also became the House of Assembly.

But emphasis is laid not on 1825 when this building was opened, but on the year 1768, when Tobago, for the first time, got a House of Assembly.

CHAPTER NINE

THE FIRST TIME TRINIDAD RECEIVED SETTLERS (1783)

T he first time Trinidad got a population of some size was following the signing of a cedula by the King of Spain in November 1783, which allowed thousands of people in the Caribbean, so long as they were Catholic, to come and settle in Trinidad.

The details of the *cedula* was the work of Roume de St. Laurent, a Frenchman who was living in Grenada at the time. It provided for grants of land and many other concessions offered to settlers if they would make their home here. It was a scheme which, as was intended, opened up the road to development for Trinidad.

And yet Roume de St Laurent might never have thought about Trinidad, had not the British captured Grenada from the French in 1762. Roume, fiercely patriotic, and who described himself at that time as "Roume, a Frenchman, living under the British yoke", was extremely unhappy, and anxious to get out of Grenada. It was just around that time that he saw a letter from a traveller inviting people to settle in Trinidad. Roume became extremely interested. The letter had made the condition that the settlers had to be Catholic, and this suited Roume, because it meant that all the French people like himself were welcome in Trinidad.

Although Spain was neutral in this war between Britain and France, both Spain and France had a common dislike for Britain. And they had another important thing in common: they were both Catholic nations. Then, too, the British war in the Windward Islands was seen by Spain as a British bid to extend its rule in the area, and so Spain was anxious to populate Trinidad and colonise it. Only so, the Spanish authorities felt, would it be strong enough to resist any onslaught from the British. The fact that because of the British war in the Windward Islands many French settlers were willing to leave and settle elsewhere fitted in well with the Spanish plan and also with the ideas of Roume de St. Laurent.

In 1777, Roume lost no time in visiting Trinidad to see for himself. He was welcomed by the governor, Manuel Falquaz, and from him he may have learnt that the island was sparsely peopled, having no more than about 2,500 Spaniards. Roume also met two Spanish engineers here, who were conducting a survey. They had been all through the island and told Roume of the complete emptiness of this beautiful country.

For Roume himself it was love at first sight. He was a naturalist and fascinated with a Trinidad that was most unspoiled and green and that had so many rare species of plant and animal life. He loved the lie of the land, the fertility of the soil, in fact, everything his eyes beheld here. He decided that he would do all in his power, not only to make Trinidad his home, but to make it a home to the thousands of French people in the Windward Islands.

Roume told Governor Falquaz of the great scheme he was devising to bring settlers here, but considering the magnitude of the scheme, the governor asked him to discuss the matter with the Intendant at Caracas, the man responsible for the *audiencia* (the Spanish administrative region) which included Trinidad. Roume went to Caracas, but he was apparently not satisfied, for it was a big decision for the Intendant to take. Roume's plan included the granting of land to settlers and many other incentives to encourage them to leave their homes and move to Trinidad. It might have entailed much discussion

PHILIPPE ROSE ROUME DE ST. LAURENT
FIRST PROMULGATED THE CEDULA OF
POPULATION OF 1783.

with the King of Spain, and thus many letters crossing the seas, and much passage of time. Therefore Roume decided to go and see the King personally and present his case.

Roume embarked, but of course no visitor could reach the King's court without invitation, and because of this fact, and the intrigues of war, and the suspicion of a Frenchman, and such matters, Roume on his way was held up more than a year in Paris before he could see the King of Spain.

But when he finally got an audience with the King, success came at once. The King was impressed with Roume's plan for the settlement of Trinidad, and based on Roume's proposal he prepared a Royal Cedula. This Royal Cedula for the Population of Trinidad was signed by the King at San Lorenzo, Spain, on 20 November, 1783. The *cedula* was brought back to Trinidad in 1784 by Don José María Chacón, who had succeeded Manuel Falquaz.

Chacón translated, published, and proclaimed the *cedula*, and it was not long afterwards that a flood of immigrants from the French Windward Islands began to pour in. This flood was swelled by immigrants from Santo Domingo who fled the troubles in that island caused by the outbreak of the French Revolution in 1789. Trinidad, which had about 2,500 people when Roume de St. Laurent came here in 1783, received about 16,000 settlers between that time and 1797, at which point the British seized the island from Spain.

CHAPTER TEN

THE FIRST TIME THE ENGLISH LANGUAGE CAME TO TRINIDAD (1797)

T he first time the English language was introduced into Trinidad was on that occasion in February 1797 when British forces under General Sir Ralph Abercromby captured this island from the Spaniards. However, at that point English was not entirely unknown in Trinidad, for under the Spanish cedula of 1783, admitting Catholic settlers, also a few British people—mainly Irish—had come in.

But the vast majority of the settlers were from the French Windward Islands, who had established French as the language of the Trinidad masses. Even though the British came in 1797, it was more than half a century afterwards that English achieved any hold on Trinidad, and the cause of the great delay was due mainly to the following reason: Abercromby had agreed to Chacón's request to maintain the existing religion, customs and culture in Trinidad as well as maintain Spanish laws.

Naturally, this had kept the French language vibrant, and added to this, not many English-speaking people cared to settle in this island which, although it had become British, had an almost entirely French-speaking population, and was under Spanish laws.

It was not until Governor Ralph Woodford came here in 1813 that English became a language of some importance, for Woodford ruled in 1814 that English be introduced into the Courts of Law. However, this did not make much of an impact on the people at large, and the language of the land remained unshakingly French.

In general, the few English people who were here were very hostile to this state of affairs for they felt their language, customs and culture were being treated as second rate, although this island was under the British Crown. They formed a party called "The English Party", and campaigned heatedly for the withdrawal of Spanish laws. As vociferous as the English Party was, it was a small group and made no immediate impact. Especially so as Woodford, who stayed in office for 15 years, seemed very favourable to Spanish laws, which incidentally gave more power to a governor than English laws did.

However, the constant pressure of the English Party was beginning to tell, and the appearance of "The Trinidad Gazette" in 1822 seemed to give a very large voice to these English settlers. By then there were many more of them than before, and they kept applying pressure, not only on the governor here, but on parliament in London.

Woodford was able to stave off their effort to a considerable extent, but when Woodford died in 1828, matters became a great deal easier for them.

However, this was the hectic period approaching the abolition of slavery, and the issue distracted everyone, but as soon as this was past the English faction was to achieve stunning success.

Slavery was abolished in 1838, and Fitzgerald Hill, who was governor here at the time, died in office in 1839. Hill had hardly had time to consider the burning issues of language, laws, customs, and culture in Trinidad, but as soon as his successor arrived here, the issues, in a manner of speaking, came to the centre of the stage. Hill's successor was the Irishman Sir Henry McLeod, and on his arrival here, he expressed surprise to find Spanish laws still so well entrenched. He said he was determined "to see the English laws in force here, and in fact to make this an English colony".

GOVERNOR SIR RALPH WOODFORD, THE FIRST
CIVIL GOVERNOR OF TRINIDAD (1813-1829)

One could imagine the glee of the English Party, who might have well called this governor their leader.

McLeod arrived in April 1840, and by June, he had had an Ordinance passed to abolish the Illustrious Cabildo, setting up in its place a Town Council of Port-of-Spain. It was a short step from that to the introduction of English Laws, which, because of a delay over which McLeod had no control, was only effected in 1844.

So far as the English Party was concerned, the introduction of English laws in 1844 was the key that opened the door. There were immediate and radical changes, and one of the chief of these affected religion, for the Catholic Church, which had remained the State Church because of the presence of Spanish laws, now saw the roles reversed, and the Anglican Church became the State Church.

The stage was set for the English language to gain the upper hand, which became more likely when Lord Harris started a system of primary schools in 1851. French and Patois, which were spoken by the masses and still very widespread, began to recede a little with the teaching of English in schools. Even today the effect of the French language, customs and culture is still with us, which has made Trinidad very much more interesting than it might have been otherwise. So looking back on all that has gone before, it is good to recall the first time that the English language came to Trinidad.

CHAPTER ELEVEN

THE FIRST SURVEY OF THE ISLAND (1797)

T he first time that Trinidad was completely surveyed and mapped was the period just following the British conquest of the island in 1797. Previous to that, the shape and size of the island were given without exact knowledge of the facts. The British wrested the island from Spain in February 1797, and at once the commander-in-chief, General Sir Ralph Abercromby, asked the captain of his surveying engineers to map the island and furnish details as to what was to be found on it.

Of course, as chief of the invading forces, Abercromby needed to report to the British authorities what their new possession was like. Especially so as the British had had no intention of assaulting Trinidad, and had considered themselves forced into doing this because the French Republicans, whom they were fighting in the Windward Islands, were finding a refuge in Trinidad.

Frederick Mallet, the captain of the surveying engineers, was directed to furnish a survey including such details as the extent of the island, its population, and how this was composed; what were its settlements and perhaps most important of all, to report on its estates—for it was its economic resources that would tell if it was worth keeping.

Mallet seemed enthusiastic to tackle the job, but had no intention of contending with the wild and forested interior. In the 1770s, Spain had sent two men here to do just this job, and Mallet decided to seek out and draw on all the information they might have got, while he himself would survey the coast. In the end he not only drew on the information the Spanish surveyors had got, but on information they had not got, for most of the interior of this first map was left blank.

It was shortly after the capitulation of Trinidad that Captain Mallet set out to survey the coastal areas, and he sailed out of Port-of-Spain bearing north and rounding the northwestern peninsula, and he made a complete journey around the island.

This survey of Captain Mallet was mainly responsible for most of the place names we have on the coast of Trinidad. Apart from giving minute details of the condition of the island, he called at every bay and inlet, and wherever he found settlers, he not only counted them and took an account of the land granted, but noted down what they told him the place was called.

Apart from this he took account of the names the Spaniards had given to certain geographical features. He wrote these down on his chart and beside them he wrote their English translations. In the agricultural areas he took details of the crops grown, the quantity of the produce, and the number of estates.

At that period almost all the settlements outside of Port-of-Spain were settlements of French planters and their slaves, and these were mainly on the coast.

The first of these that Mallet met after going through the *Boca de Monos* (or "Apes' Mouth", as he notes) was a settlement at the mouth of a river which the Spaniards had called *Madamas*. This river was so named because of the women who were always washing clothes in the river. At that point on his map Mallet wrote: *Rio de Madamas*, and beside the Spanish name he wrote: "Ladies River". Maybe because of this the French settlers who lived there gave the place a name—a name which was just a translation of what Mallet had written. They called it *Blanchisseuse*, which literally means "washer-woman".

As Mallet sailed on he encountered a few geographical features and he wrote down on his map what the Spaniards had called them. Among these were *Punta de Rio Grande*, which the French later translated to *Grand Riviere*; and *Punta de Sincuidado*, beside which he wrote "Carefree Point", his English translation. This is the place the French later called *Sans Souci*, meaning the same thing.

At the eastern tip of the north coast, he found a fairly large settlement, and this settlement had retained its Amerindian name. Apparently the Spaniards, who had met large numbers of Amerindians here and had collected them in a nearby mission, never liked changing names already there. This place was called *Toco*, and it was "Toco" that Mallet wrote down on his map.

Not too far away, down the eastern coast, there was a point to which the Spaniards had been in the custom of taking supplies in their cargo boats, called *balandras*. On his map, Mallet gave this place the name: Balandra.

Sailing further south along the east coast, Captain Mallet encountered an expansive bay with settlers all along its seaboard. Again the Spaniards had not disturbed its Arawak name: it was called Mayaro. Mallet landed here, took a census of the people, made a record of every parcel of land granted, noted the flourishing estates of cotton, coffee, and sugar, and set sail again. It was at his next stop that he made his historic mistake, for he now came to the headland that Christopher Columbus had named *Punta de la Galea* meaning "Point of the Galley". But curiously enough, Mallet wrote on his map for this point *Punta de la Golgota*, which appeared on later maps as Point Galeota.

(Another interesting fact the meaning of Galeota is very close to Columbus' name. *Galea* means galley, for Columbus said he felt the point resembled a galley under sail. Galeota is the name of a certain type of galley.)

Just off this point, in the sea, Mallet seems to have seen a jet of tar spiralling in the air, for in an account he mentions that this often occurs here at certain seasons of the year. On his map, at the place indicated, he writes "Gulf or whirlpool".

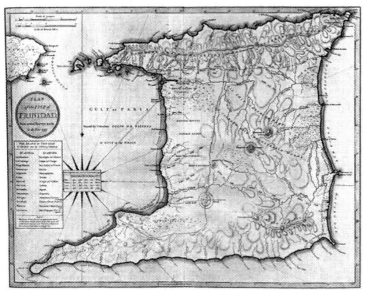

MAP OF TRINIDAD MADE FROM ACTUAL SURVEYS IN 1797

Mallet made many more interesting observations. For instance, when he came to the western tip of the south coast, he saw a profusion of shrubs on the sandy marsh, and at once he wrote on his map for this feature "Marsh of Icaque". He must have been told that the shrubs were of the kind known as "icaque" to the French settlers. This shrub, of the rosaceous family, was known as *icacos* to the Spaniards, and in fact this is what the area came to be called, Icacos.

As Mallet rounded the point and turned northward into the Gulf of Paria, he came upon a bay lined with giant cedars, and naturally the settlers there must have informed him that the Spaniards had named the place after those trees. On his map, where this bay was located, he wrote "Bay of Cedars", and on the headland in front of him *Punta del Cedro*—the Spanish version of "Cedar Point". Later, the coast of the bay of cedars took on the name of Cedros, which is Spanish for cedars.

Mallet arrived back in Port-of-Spain that July, and his map contained most of the names by which we call coastal villages today. He recorded copious details, such as details of population, crops, production, and types of soil.

CHAPTER TWELVE

THE FIRST FEW STREETS (1797)

T he first street in Trinidad was the roadway that ran along the waterfront of the seaside village, Puerto de España, a place later to be known as Port-of-Spain. Just in front of it was the little military battery, Fort San Andres, the ruins of which can still be seen.

The Spaniards named this roadway *Calle de la Marina*, and the waterfront was *Plaza de la Marina*. When the British captured Trinidad from the Spaniards in 1797, they simply translated the words *Plaza de la Marina* to Marine Square. Incidentally, the name Marine Square remained until 1961, when it was changed to Independence Square.

There are few records of the period which describe what Port-of-Spain looked like, or even mentions this first street, but one occasion when this scene was the subject was on a day in 1777 when Roume de St. Laurent visited Trinidad for the first time. (Roume de St. Laurent was the man who devised the well-known measures leading to the Cedula of Population, which brought thousands of French planters and their slaves to Trinidad.)

Writing of that first visit Roume de St. Laurent says: "It is on the West Coast that the Spaniards settle themselves, at the place where one lands, called *Puerto de España*. Here there are several guns in a battery . . . a church, and about eighty houses plastered with a mixture of mud and grass, then white-washed with lime-wash and covered with thatch. The Governor lives here."

These eighty tapia houses would have stood behind the waterfront and in front of them would have been this street, or roadway, *Calle de la Marina*. The church mentioned would have been a wooden, ramshackle Roman Catholic church in what is now called Tamarind Square.

Roume adds, "The Governor lives here", because it was unusual for the Governor not to live in the capital, which in 1777 was still San José. Roume stayed as a guest with Governor Manual Falquaz.

At this point there were no other streets, but when Governor José María Chacón came here in 1784 to replace Falquaz, a great deal of development was about to take place because of Roume de St. Laurent's visit. He liked Trinidad so much, and realised that the island was so sparsely populated (only about three thousand Spaniards in all, and the Arawaks of course he could not see) that he devised a scheme for the immigration into this island of the Caribbean French. He took the scheme personally to the court of the King of Spain at Madrid, and the King, impressed with Roume's proposals, proclaimed the famous Cedula of Population for Trinidad on 20 November, 1783.

Manuel Falquaz, who had been governor of Trinidad, had died since 1779, but it was only now the King of Spain was ready to send out someone to replace him. He had named José María Chacón as the new governor, and Chacón, who brought the Cedula document here, arrived in 1784.

By the British conquest of 1797 there were already thousands of Caribbean French people here, comprising French planters and their slaves. Of these, a good number had settled in *Puerto de España*—now Port-of-Spain—and, as expected, they constructed the first few streets.

The British made ten streets in Port-of-Spain, and these were the following: running from north to south, the most easterly was called *Calle del Infante*. The French had had their own names for all the streets and they called this one *Rue des Trois Chandelles*. The British named this Duncan Street, after Admiral Adam Duncan.

The next street was *Calle del Principe*, which the French called *Rue l'Eglise*. The British named this street Nelson Street, to honour Admiral Lord Nelson.

Then came *Calle San José*, sometimes called *Calle de Mercado* or Market Street, as the town's market was on that street. The French saw this as a Market Street too, calling it *Rue de la Place*. The British called it George Street after reigning monarch George III.

After *Calle San José* was *Calle Santa Ana*, for its northern side tended to follow the course of the *Rio Santa Ana* or St. Ann's River. The French name reflected the same idea, for they called it *Rue Sainte Anne*. The British called this street Charlotte Street, after Charlotte, the wife of George III.

The next street was *Calle de Herrera*, Herrera apparently being the name of a police chief. The French called this street *Rue Neuve*. The British, in what seemed to be another gesture to royalty, called it Henry Street.

The last street was *Calle San Carlos*, called by the French *Rue des Anglais*, because of a brawl between British soldiers and French republicans in that street in 1796. The British named it Frederick Street, after the father of George III.

The other street was just in the process of being built. Chacón in 1785 had had the *Rio Santa Ana* (St. Ann's River) diverted, and now that the old bed was being filled up it was taking shape as a street. The British named this street after Chacón, calling it Chacon Street.

Of the streets running from east to west, the first one, coming from the sea, was *Calle de la Marina*, which was *Rue de la Marine* to the French, and which the English called King Street. The second was *Calle San Luis*, which name the French accepted in that they called it *Rue St. Louis*. The English called it Queen Street.

Passing Queen Street, the next cross-street was *Calle Santa Rosa*, which again the French accepted, translating the name to *Rue Sainte Rose*. The British, in their patriotic frame of mind, called it Prince Street.

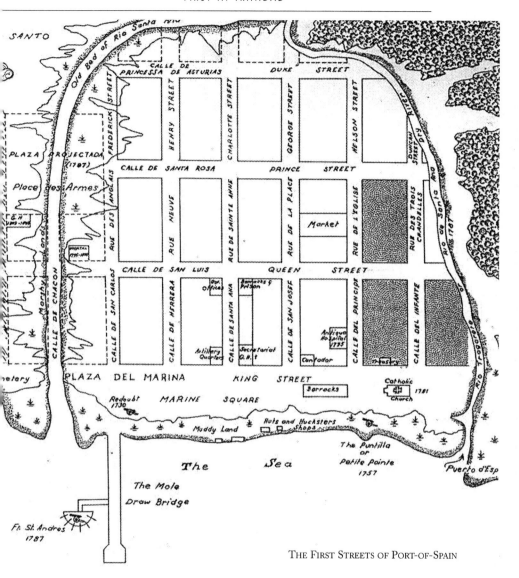

THE FIRST STREETS OF PORT-OF-SPAIN

The last cross-street to the north was *Calle Princesa de Asturias*. There doesn't seem to have been a French name for this street, but the British completed their patriotic picture by calling this road-way Duke Street.

These were the first few streets in Port-of-Spain.

THIRTEEN
CHAPTER
THE FIRST POLICE FORCE (1797)

I t is interesting that the first police force in Trinidad should
have been set up by one of the toughest governors that
Trinidad has ever had—Lieutenant-Colonel Sir Thomas
Picton, the first British governor of Trinidad.

Because Trinidad's first police force was set up by Picton does not
mean that under Spanish rule there had been no system of keeping
law and order. This was certainly not the case. The Spanish system of
keeping law and order here could not have been considered a police
service in the way that we understand it. Under the Spanish system,
the *Alguazil Mayor* had the function of maintaining law and order,
but his general duties, as well as the duties of the other *alguazils*
under him, were not confined to keeping law and order alone. Also
appointed by the Illustrious Cabildo of Port-of-Spain, their areas of
operation were essentially within the limits of the town. The
Illustrious Cabildo was, in essence, a Town Council.

When the British seized Trinidad from the Spaniards in 1797, the
commander of the British forces, Sir Ralph Abercromby, left his aide-
de-camp, Thomas Picton, in charge with the words: "I have placed you
in a trying and delicate position, nor . . . can I leave you a strong
garrison; but I shall give you ample powers. Execute Spanish law as
well as you can. Do justice according to your conscience, and that is all
that can be expected of you."

Nobody knew better than Picton that he was being left in a trying and delicate position. Of the population of 18,000 people, no fewer than 15,000 were French republicans, as hostile to British rule as they had been to the former Spanish administration. They were a greater danger now, for at least Spain was an ally, and as objectionable to them as Spain was, being royalist, it was the very Spanish Crown that had given them the right to settle in Trinidad. And even though they had had their differences with Spain, Spain and France were two Catholic nations, and were therefore closely linked.

The French republicans were bitter enemies of the English because the English had sided with royalist France and were fighting a war against the French republicans in the Windward Islands. Indeed, many thousands of the French republicans in Trinidad at that time were people who had fled the bloody battles of that war. Some had come to lie low and plot, and perhaps return to harass the English. So the French republicans had reacted angrily to the British capture of Trinidad. They decided to make Picton's regime as tumultuous and as perilous as possible.

Picton, for his part, could not have been more equal to the challenge. In temperament, he was just the man to step into the fray, eager to "fight fire with fire". An example of Picton's attitude was that he erected some gallows just in front of Government House, and he carried out his brand of justice with despatch and without what he would have called the humbug of trial. Those gallows never languished for lack of use.

Quite apart from this, it was no secret that Picton was capable of great cruelty. The famous instance to cite would be the case of Luisa Calderon, a child of about 12 years, whom he tortured by having her hung from the roof by one hand to induce her to confess a theft.

It could well be that the establishment of the police force was one of the first constitutional measures he took so far as the establishment of law and order was concerned. But take it he did. He is said to have appointed a Police Chief, and to have given him a force of eight men to start with. And this was the beginning of the police force that we have today.

CHAPTER FOURTEEN

THE FIRST NEWSPAPERS (1799 TO THE 1860s)

T he first newspaper in Trinidad was published very early in the British days. It was the Trinidad Courant, and its first edition appeared on 1 August, 1799.

The title was significant, for although it was carrying the banner of the ruling English, the French term *courant* could not but have appealed to the French-speaking masses, who at that time were more than ninety percent of the total population. The term courant, too, must have inspired confidence, for it implied that it was in possession of all the facts.

The Trinidad Courant was a weekly, and even so, it was a comparatively small news sheet. It was very much a government gazette, and amidst the very scanty news of the day, and copious advertisements, government notices, proclamations, and ordinances were very much in evidence. Everything was published in English and French. The news to a great extent reflected the uneasy peace which confronted Governor Sir Thomas Picton in that period. The constant threat of a Spanish counter-attack from across the main and the turmoil from both without and within created by the French republicans provided Picton with what was perhaps the most trying time of his life. Picton was not slow to string up offenders on the gallows he had built in front of Government House, and he must have been glad to have the Trinidad Courant in order to make known to all men, through his notices and proclamations, that he would meet violence with violence in order to preserve British rule.

As for the advertisements in the Trinidad Courant, mostly they concerned estates for sale, and notices of runaway slaves.

The Trinidad Courant seemed to grow more and more into an instrument of the government, and by the time Picton left in 1802 it could have easily been called a "Royal Gazette"— the official organ of British colonial governments.

Maybe the biggest event ever reported by the Trinidad Courant was the complete destruction of Port-of-Spain by the great fire of 1808. The fire took place on Thursday, 24 March, 1808, and on Friday, 1st April, the Trinidad Courant reported: "The terror which took possession of the unfortunate tenants and proprietors of this neighbourhood is not to be described, nor can fancy paint a scene of such astonishment and dismay."

The Trinidad Courant went on to provide certain details of the destruction caused by the fire and its report guided the British Members of Parliament when the time came to vote money for the rebuilding of the town. In some cases its report conflicted with that of Sir Thomas Hislop, who was governor here at the time.

The great fire wreaked complete destruction on Port-of-Spain, but the Trinidad Courant survived to tell the story of those early years. And it was not until the year 1822, long after the administrations of Picton and Hislop, and in the comparatively placid era of Sir Ralph Woodford, that this the first newspaper in Trinidad came to the end of its day. Or maybe it was just the name that came to an end. It had been the only newspaper all through the years from 1799 to 1822, and therefore was heavily relied upon by the government to publish its edicts and notices. Unlike Picton's time, this was not a period of fire and sword. Apart from the proclamations on the slave question—a storm which was just beginning to brew—many of Woodford's notices had to do with balls at his cottage "St. Ann's".

Anyway, the year is now 1822, and in the continued absence of an official government gazette, we see the end of the Trinidad Courant and the beginning of another newspaper—the Trinidad Gazette. But the Trinidad Gazette itself did not last very long. In September 1825 it left the scene, giving way to a new journal, the Port-of-Spain Gazette. The Port-of-Spain Gazette, which was not to have a rival until 1838, was to outlast all the newspapers of the 19th century, and come right into the mid-20th century.

The newspapers which came on the scene in 1838 to rival the Port-of-Spain Gazette was the ultra-British Trinidad Standard, a paper extremely concerned with the future of the estates and the prospect of labour. The year 1838, it will be recalled, was the very year slavery was abolished, but of course the labour crisis had been looming since before Emancipation. The Trinidad Standard lasted only until 1847.

All the newspapers so far had backed the government and the land-owning class, and indeed, the Port-of-Spain Gazette was openly described as a government newspaper.

But in 1849 came a newspaper with a difference. This was a newspaper which by its name declared where it stood, and the fearlessness of its editor knew no match. This was The Trinidadian, and its editor was the out-spoken radical Numa des Sources. Des Sources saw the establishment as favouring all the white outsiders who came here at the expense of the Trinidadian. He decided to speak out. He frontally attacked Lord Harris, accusing him of favouritism and of class discrimination, declaring that the British officials and their hangers-on had no interests whatsoever in Trinidad and the Trinidadian. It was not surprising that this paper could not last long. It bowed out in 1853, just before Lord Harris left.

But although there were other rivals to the Port-of-Spain Gazette, this newspaper was by now well entrenched. It seemed to be flourishing uninterruptedly, while the Trinidad Spectator arrived on the scene in 1845 and left in 1848, and while the Trinidad Herald, which appeared in 1853, ceased publication the very next year. In fact, the Port-of-Spain Gazette saw fourteen newspapers come and go before the century ended. Among these newspapers were: The Trinidad

Press, The Sentinel, The Colonist, Star of the West, The Chronicle, New Era, The Echo, The Telegraph, The Trinidad Palladium, Public Opinion, and The San Fernando Gazette.

In the main, they had claimed to be independent in outlook, but in reality most went with the tide of planter opinion, especially *The Colonist* and *The Telegraph*. Very few were really radical and championing the cause of the people, but the outstanding one in this role was *The Sentinel*, which seemed a true sentinel of the rights of the black masses. This newspaper was also short-lived; it appeared in 1856 and went out in 1863.

These were the first newspapers to appear on the scene from 1799—shortly after the advent of the British—up to the end of the nineteenth century.

CHAPTER FIFTEEN

OUR FIRST GREAT ARTIST (1813-1888)

O ur first great artist—the man who put us in the picture, in a manner of speaking—was the first and the finest water-colour painter ever to emerge in this country.

This was Michel Jean Cazabon. There have been many fine water-colour painters in Trinidad, for example, his contemporary, Theodora Walter, and the late Edwin Hing Wan, but Michel Jean was unique.

Born in 1813, the place of his birth seems to have been San Fernando. His parents, both mulattoes, came here from Martinique, and it is almost certain they had come as part of the influx of Caribbean French settlers here under the Cedula of Population.

1813 was also the year Governor Sir Ralph Woodford arrived, and Michel Jean, who was already 15 when Woodford departed, seems to have been as conscious of the appearance of his environment as this governor was. Cazabon, in fact, had left Trinidad long before this governor did. At the age of nine, he was sent to the town of Ware in Hertfordshire, England, to go to school—which seems to tell us that his parents were not as poor and humble as is often said. As a young man, he went over to Paris to study medicine, but, curiously enough, he could not stand the sight of blood. So he reverted to a boyhood love— painting—and in this he showed a preference for water-colours.

Therefore it would not at all have been surprising if, on his return to Trinidad in 1841, his parents (if they were alive then) had taken issue with him. What sort of profession was this? Was it reasonable to leave medicine to dabble in water-colours? And he was already 28 anyway. He had spent 19 years abroad and instead of returning as a qualified medical doctor, he had returned home with a wife and a few empty canvases!

But as it turned out, that was just as well, for had he qualified as a medical doctor it is extremely unlikely that we would have been discussing him at all. Even if he had been an exceptional doctor he would hardly have been the first in Trinidad. On the other hand, the outstanding work of Cazabon as an artist has set him apart from most of the artists who have gone before.

In 1841, Cazabon, apart from setting out to put us into the picture, was getting set to do some of the invaluable work of his life. Whether he knew it or not, he was going to be a recorder in water-colours.

Seeing Trinidad for the first time since childhood, he went all over the country, painting the scenes before his eyes. The result of this was that the work of his brush on canvas is about the only evidence we have of what Trinidad was like around the middle of the nineteenth century. These paintings come in two categories. It is not, for example, the charm of his painting of Mount Tamana from the Arima heights that excites us, nor is it the rich lushness of his painting of the road to the Pitch Lake. These paintings are beautiful, but the scene is unchanging, and so we remain simply admiring the great work. Some of his other paintings have both beauty and historic importance. For example, the historic change that has come over the Port-of-Spain waterfront can only be appreciated by looking at Cazabon's "King's Wharf and South Quay".

When Cazabon painted this picture, South Quay had just been constructed after land had been reclaimed from the sea. That project had been completed in 1832. Beyond the crowd in Cazabon's picture is Fort San Andres in the distance, which in that period was seeing its first days as part of the mainland. Before, it had been an off-shore island. To the right of Fort San Andres, and in the further distance, we see the lighthouse, built in 1842, very shortly after Cazabon's return.

However, the most dramatic point about this picture, and which tends to make us gasp, is that Fort San Andres, which is the home of the Police Traffic Branch today, is on the water's edge! So although we look at Cazabon's strange crowd of fisher-folk on the wharf, the cart with the casks of rum nearby, and the general quaintness, and realise we are deep in the nineteenth century. It is the fact that South Quay was on the water's edge that excites us, for it is nothing of the sort today.

Among the scores of other paintings that Cazabon did in the mid-1840s, he painted one of Trinity Church in or just after 1844 —the year that English laws came to Trinidad. We know it was painted then because it was on the advent of English laws that Trinity Church became the State Church, and in this picture, in one of the front columns, there is a badge to show it. This picture could not have been painted much later for it appears in his lithograph album " 18 Views of Trinidad", printed and produced in Paris in 1851.

This album was the first set of Cazabon's pictures that went out into the world, and at once marked Cazabon as one of the fine water-colour painters of his time. It also presented Cazabon to us, as well as show the world what Trinidad was like at that time. Or even if we do not put it that way—for Cazabon did not paint everything—his water-colour pictures gave to the world very many glimpses of the Trinidad of the mid-nineteenth century.

For all his great talent Cazabon never seemed to have become well-to-do. He seemed also to have been very shy and retiring, although

VIEW OF PORT-OF-SPAIN BY MICHEL-JEAN CAZABON

not too shy to have the following advertisement in the newspapers during 1850: "Michel Cazabon, drawing master, portrait and landscape painter in oils and water-colours. Mr. Cazabon avails himself of the end of the year to return his thanks for the liberal support he has hitherto received from the admirers of the art and begs to inform them that the better to meet the convenience of students, he will attend either privately or in classes ..."

The charge for this tuition was $5.00 a month, per pupil taught privately twice a week, and $3.00 a month for each pupil in a class.

He apparently went to Martinique, his parent's country, some time in the mid-1860s, and when he returned he got an appointment as art master at Queen's Royal College, then in the Princes Building. There he had the reputation of being a very "soft" master, a teacher to be made fun of by his students.

But by that time his reputation had grown immensely, for he had had a second album of lithographs published in Paris, and had confirmed his reputation not only as an artist of exceptional talent, but as a great recorder of the Trinidad scene.

Cazabon continued his fine work until the year 1888, when he died. The great beauty of his paintings will, of course, always have undying appeal, but their historic nature becomes more precious with every passing day. The more Trinidad changes the more priceless his work will become, and it is safe to say that the name of Michel Jean Cazabon will always be enshrined in Trinidad's history.

CHAPTER SIXTEEN

THE FIRST RECREATION GROUND (1817)

When Governor Sir Ralph Woodford, shortly after his arrival here in 1813, left the leaking, ramshackle Government House in which he had taken up office, the question of a recreation ground for the people of Port-of-Spain could hardly have been on his mind.

But this was exactly what resulted from his search for a new Government House.

He was forced to leave the one he had entered in 1813, not only because the house was ramshackle and leaking, but also because there were problems associated with his occupancy of the house. The house, which was on the site that the Port-of-Spain Hilton Hotel occupies today, was the country house of Governor Thomas Hislop before the great Port-of-Spain fire of 1808. Hislop retired to it for an office as well as for a home, after the official Government House had been burnt down, and when Hislop left Trinidad in 1811, first William Munro and then Ralph Woodford assumed office in it. This house, called "Belmont" by Hislop, was not owned by the government—only rented. The property was claimed by the heirs of early settlers called Edward Barry and Black. Barry was said to have bought the land since 1785, but owing to a dispute with another settler, administration of the property was in the hands of the court. Woodford, as governor, declared that no proper papers had been granted by the Spanish government and so the property had reverted to the Crown. The Barry faction fought him relentlessly, even taking the matter to the Privy Council. The Privy Council declared against Woodford, and he had to give up. And now developed the circumstances which gained for the townsfolk their first recreation ground.

When the lawsuit over "Belmont" had first started, Woodford, uncertain as to the outcome, had begun to look for a new Government House. He had shown an interest in the property known as Champs Elysées, a property in Maraval that at the time belonged to Rose de Gannes, mother of Roume de St. Laurent. Insufficient funds in the Treasury had prevented him from buying it, but when funds improved, this property was no longer for sale. It was then that Woodford had a second look at a property he had seen before. He had seen it every day, in fact, for he had only to look down from the ramshackle "Belmont House" upon the old abandoned estate not too far below him. This was the old Paradise Estate, at this time owned by the heirs of Madame Henri Peschier. Woodford offered the heirs the sum of £6,000, which was accepted, and he came into the possession of the entire estate, comprising two parcels of land, amounting to 232 acres in all. Out of this land, though, the heirs of Madame Peschier reserved a small piece of ground where the other Peschiers were buried. This was to be a family burial ground.

When cleared, it was this former estate which became the Queen's Park, as it was officially called, or the Grand Savannah, which was its popular name. Woodford had 219 acres of the 232 acres laid out "for the pasturage of cows and for the recreation of the townsfolk", but because it was so far from the town it was hardly used for the recreation of the townsfolk, but mainly used as a government pasture.

(To give an idea of how far the Queen's Park or Grand Savannah was from Port-of-Spain: when Woodford bought the old Paradise Estate there was little of the town north of Park Street, which could have been taken as Port-of-Spain's northern limit. The rest was countryside, and as was shown, nearby "Belmont House" was considered a country house.)

Although the principal reason for purchasing the estate was to find a site for Government House, Woodford did not build on it. In 1819, an estate lying north of the Queen's Park was for sale and this Woodford quickly bought on behalf of the Cabildo. And it was on these grounds—the grounds of the former Hollandais Estate—that he renovated the building that was going to be the new Government House. This was the Hollandais estate house which Woodford then called "St. Ann's Cottage". Near to this site, the present mansion was constructed in 1876, which was to become the home of all succeeding governors since that time. This is the present-day President's House, which was started by Governor James Robert Longden in 1873 and completed in the time of Governor Sir Henry Turner Irving. Irving opened it just after Easter in 1876.

But to return to our first recreation ground. The Queen's Park or Grand Savannah did not prove itself much of a centre for recreation until many years later, when the town crept right up to it. Yet to some extent it did attract the townsfolk, and from early on too, as can be seen in this water-colour painting by Michel Jean Cazabon. Apart from the cows grazing, we can see two women obviously in gossip; and we can see an old man probably coaching his grandson on how to fly a kite.

The Queen's Park, or the Grand Savannah, later to be called the Queen's Park Savannah, only came into regular use as a ground for the recreation of the townsfolk after a grandstand was erected there in 1854 and races were held every Christmas. This was the start of the Christmas Race Meeting of the Trinidad Turf Club. Activities increased and the Queen's Park Savannah became livened up with cricket, especially after the Queen's Park Cricket Club was formed towards the end of the 19th century, and after the Bonanza Stores started a cricket competition there in the 1890s.

When the 20th century opened, the Queen's Park Savannah was very much a centre for the recreation of the townsfolk as was originally envisaged, but it had receded as a pasturage as was very much the case in the next few decades, when motor traffic began making animal traffic the obsolete thing that it is today.

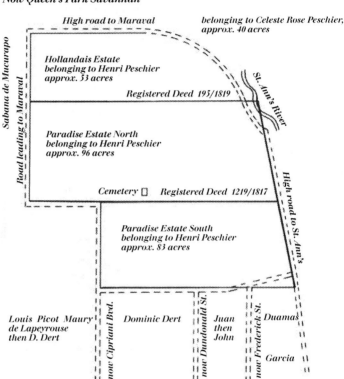

Paradise Estates and Hollandais Estate (1782)
Now Queen's Park Savannah

However, up to the late 1920s the Queen's Park Savannah was termed "Government Pasture", and there were fees laid down for the pasturage of animals.

The "pasturage" aspect of the Queen's Park Savannah is a thing of the past, and it is difficult to imagine today a ground that could be more of a centre of recreation for the townsfolk. At all hours of the day there are games being played on the Queen's Park Savannah, and from morning to night, especially on mornings and at nights, there are crowds of people—young and old—jogging and exercising around the Savannah to keep fit. It is at Carnival time that it knows its brightest moments as far as recreation is concerned. At this time, thousands of people throng the green acres for the Panorama steelband competition, for Dimanche Gras, for children's Carnival shows, and for the parade of the Carnival bands. Woodford's purchase of 1817 has certainly proved worthwhile.

CHAPTER *SEVENTEEN*

T HE   F IRST   S ECONDARY   S CHOOL   (1 8 3 6)

T he first secondary school in Trinidad was founded in Port-of-Spain in the year 1836.

This was St. Joseph's Convent, and an advertisement in the Port-of-Spain Gazette which appeared for several days during February 1836, said: "The Ladies of St. Joseph have the honour to inform the heads of families that their establishment will be opened on the First of March. Those persons who are desirous of placing their children in the establishment are invited to apply to the ladies themselves for such information as they may require. Their prospectus will be published immediately, and will explain both the plan and the terms of tuition, and they trust by their care and zeal to render themselves worthy of confidence." And this was signed: "Madame D'Heureux's house, St. James Street". On the appointed day, the school was opened by Madame de la Croix.

In this way the Little Sisters of the Order of St. Joseph de Cluny announced the establishment of St. Joseph's Convent in Port-of-Spain. They had arrived in Trinidad that very year, and so they had wasted no time at all in offering their services to the community. As was shown, the Convent saw its beginning in Madame D'Heureux's house in St. James Street, which today is part of Frederick Street. (At first, Frederick Street ran only as far north as the northern end of Woodford Square. Then the town was extended to Park Street, and at that time the prolongation of Frederick Street to Park Street was known as St. James Street.) The Convent stayed in Madame D'Heureux's house until 1840, by which year it appeared that so many girls were attending it that the Sisters of St. Joseph de Cluny decided they would have to build a Convent. Or maybe constructing their own building was the intention from the start. However it was, in 1840 the Convent went to its present site on Pembroke Street— that part of which was then known as Kent Street.

The Convent quickly established a reputation for sound teaching, and what was seen as most important, moulding the young girls into excellent young ladies. So much was this so that in the very year, 1840, the Catholics decided that their young men, too, must benefit from a secondary education, and a Catholic college for boys was opened not far from the Convent, on what was then Cumberland Street. (This is part of Abercromby Street today.) Incidentally, these two institutions sharpened the rivalry between the Catholics and the Anglicans, and led to the establishment of Queen's Collegiate, to be superceded by Queen's Royal College.

To return to the subject of St. Joseph's Convent: the pupils paid a small fee to assist in the running of the Convent. Girls of slender means were never turned away, however. These girls never received the subjects on the prospectus—which were reading, writing, and arithmetic—but they were taught needlework and in general benefitted from being in such a genteel environment.

It could be said that when St. Joseph's Convent was founded in March 1836, it stood out like a beacon in education, lighting up not only its own surroundings, but the future of higher learning in Trinidad.

CHAPTER EIGHTEEN

THE FIRST TIME THE LABOURING CLASS BECAME FREE (1838)

T he first time that the labouring class in Trinidad became free was on the 1 August, 1838, the day slavery was abolished.

Ever since 1710, when the Dutch had sold African slaves to Trinidad planters, the conditions of the labouring class had been one of serfdom. Before 1710, the population of Spaniards in Trinidad was so tiny that one could not speak of a labouring class.

Perhaps it could be said that a well-organised system of slavery coincided with the influx into Trinidad of Caribbean French settlers and their slaves just after the declaration of the Cedula of Population in 1783. From the period of the arrival of the first of these settlers — which would not have been before early 1785 — to the time of the British conquest of 1797, approximately 1,000 planters had brought in some 16,000 slaves.

There was constant agitation among the slaves towards gaining their freedom and as the 19th century opened, there was a great deal of agitation in the British Parliament also, in the matter of bringing about a change in the condition of slavery.

In 1821, Governor Sir Ralph Woodford was charged with introducing certain measures which would lighten the burden of slavery. This particular Order-in-Council from the British government made two clear points: (1) that there should be no compulsory labour on Sundays, and (2) it prohibited the punishment of any female slave "by means of whips, cat-o-nine tails, or sticks". But it allowed the use of the stocks or any other punishment which the governor might authorise. (The stocks were contraptions with holes through which the hands and feet, and sometimes the head, were placed and kept there rigidly for punishment.)

The slave-owners found it an outrage that they could not punish their slaves as they wished, but the Order-in-Council had to be adhered to and, as was said, the road to freedom had taken a significant turn. There was increasing pressure in the British parliament, mainly by William Wilberforce and Thomas Fowel Buxton, who headed an anti-slavery group. The influence of this group, and maybe subtle economic considerations, so dominated slavery affairs that on 28 August, 1833, the British parliament passed an act which declared "that slavery shall be abolished throughout the British Colonies on, from, and after, the First of August, 1834".

But slavery was not really abolished on that date.

According to the Act, from 1 August, 1834, all slaves were to become "apprenticed labourers". Those who were working in the fields or in factories were to serve a further six years, after which they were to be absolutely free. House slaves, such as domestic workers, were to serve four years. For "slaves under the age of six", freedom would come on 1 August, 1834.

So 1 August, 1834, which is known as Emancipation Day, was freedom day only for the baby slaves. The labouring class was not satisfied with this and there was agitation throughout the land. Amidst the threat of widespread disorder, the Port-of-Spain Gazette declared on 18 July, 1834: "Now apprentices are bound to work for their masters when and where their masters please, for five or six years, at the end of which time they are able to work and provide for themselves. Now, this is your case. It is to enable you to provide for yourselves that the King has thought proper to bind you apprentices for six years ..."

But the slaves would have none of that, and when day broke on 1 August, 1834, the country was thrown into turmoil. Thousands of slaves left their estates and marched to Port-of-Spain. In front of Government House they stood in the rain, crying: "Pas de six ans! Pas de six ans!" (No six years!)

The governor called out the militia, while numbers of planters and businessmen roamed the streets with their guns.

The slaves, now called apprentices, milled around Government House, and when Governor Fitzgerald Hill came out on the balcony and tried to explain the position he was hooted down. The militia, apparently afraid of a riot, did not then try to disperse the slaves.

But the next day the slaves, who had not returned to their estates, continued to mill around Government House, and this time things took a serious turn when Governor Hill, going out to inspect the militia, was reportedly followed by a menacing crowd. Many were arrested and sentenced on the spot, and now the cavalry and picket guards charged to clear the street. The atmosphere was tense.

However, by Sunday, most of the slaves, resigned, returned to their estates, and the Port-of-Spain Gazette reported: "We are happy to say that tranquillity has been restored in Port-of-Spain and that the accounts from the various districts throughout the island are satisfactory."

The people seemed to have decided to wait.

However, developments in the other islands did not show that the workers there were going to be as patient. There was such unrest and agitation that the legislatures in St. Lucia, St. Vincent, Grenada and Barbados, all voted to free their so-called apprentices on 1 August, 1838. In other words, in four years instead of six. The governor of St. Vincent, George Tyler, said to a crowd of these workers on 11 May, 1838: "You will soon hear that on this day a law has passed the Legislature making every one of you free on the First of August."

The slaves in Trinidad clamoured for the same treatment but Governor Hill said he could not take that step as Trinidad and Tobago was a Crown Colony and had no independent House of Assembly as was the case in each of the other islands. He went to estates all over the island calling on workers to take heart and wait until 1840, when they would be free. Wherever he went, he met with hostility and the

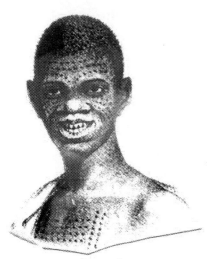

SLAVES BROUGHT FROM AFRICA TO THE CARIBBEAN OFTEN HAD TRIBAL MARKS CUT INTO THEIR SKIN.

threat of insurrection. Yet he must have had great faith in his ability to keep law and order, for on 10 July, 1838, less than a month before the slaves in the other islands were due to obtain their freedom, Governor Hill published the following proclamation: "Her Majesty the Queen and her Parliament have determined to continue the law that the praedial apprenticeship shall be observed until 1840".

The threat of serious insurrection grew to such an extent that Governor Hill urgently consulted his Council of Government. The Council of Government pleaded it had no powers to over-ride the British Emancipation Act which had stipulated that apprenticeship should be six years. In a dramatic development, with just one week to go before 1 August, 1838, the Council met in an emergency session, and the governor placed before it a proclamation for approval. Five members of the Council voted for the proclamation and five voted against it, and the governor saved the day by casting his vote for it. The proclamation read: "Be it therefore enacted and it is hereby enacted and ordained by his Excellency the Right Honourable Sir George Fitzgerald Hill, with the advice and consent of the Council of Government, that all persons who on the first day of August 1838 shall find themselves in a state of apprenticeship as praedial apprenticed labourers ... shall upon and from and after the first day of August, 1838, become and be for all intents and purposes whatsoever, absolutely and forever manumitted and set free."

So by just one vote and with just one week to go, slavery was abolished in Trinidad in 1838, and the labouring classes were set free.

CHAPTER NINETEEN

FIRST CARNIVAL OF THE STREETS IN TRINIDAD (1839)

T he first Carnival of the streets in Trinidad must have occurred on the Carnival days of the year 1839—the first Carnival at which the masses found themselves free and therefore able to participate.

The French planters who had begun establishing themselves in Trinidad a few decades before had never celebrated Carnival in any spectacular way, yet they had done enough to fire the imagination of their slaves. When these people, the black masses, became free in 1838, Carnival was clearly destined not to be the same again.

The French planters had celebrated Carnival with dainty masked balls in their great houses, and no doubt the slaves had looked on, fascinated. This went on throughout the years, from the end of the eighteenth century—when the French immigration into Trinidad started—to the abolition of slavery in 1838. Although the English captured Trinidad in 1797, British customs and culture had made little impact, because the Trinidad population had continued to be overwhelmingly French. The French-speaking people, made up of planters and slaves, formed more than 95 percent of the population, which stood at 18,000. By 1838, this ratio had not altered much. The population was nearly 40,000, but about the same proportion of the population followed the customs and culture of the French.

So it was the French culture that prevailed, and in terms of race it was the black masses who prevailed after slavery. As compared to their numbers, the population of the French planters and other whites were negligible. The free participation of the black masses in the Carnival of 1839 must have made it the most spectacular Carnival seen up to that time. The human tide must have seemed a flood of revelry.

It is interesting that the slaves did not only try to portray the dainty French dances, like the piquet and the quadrille, but brought to bear many images from the memories of the African past—the ritual masks and dances, which may have always been kept alive in the barrack yards. And to be sure, disguising was not always for an innocent purpose, for it must have been most convenient to take revenge under the cover of a mask.

But the great feature of Carnival 1839 must have been the singing and dancing in the street, something that was taking place in earnest for the first time. And there must have been the wild scenes of bongo, and stick-fighting, of moko jumbies on stilts, and countless manifestations of African gods and rituals, while the streets rang with the voices crying out the refrains in a language that was a sort of African French or French African.

And of course that year being 1839 it would have meant that English culture would have had its effect too. Because of the overwhelming number of the French-speaking people the English language could not have made much of an impact, but it must have slightly influenced the singing in the street.

At any rate the Patois being rendered by the singers in 1839 was certainly going to last well over one hundred years. However, the Carnival, as was being laid down by those first revellers, was destined to grow and flourish and become a big part of the culture of Trinidad. We know that those two days did not provide colour and spectacle. This was to come. What they did was to take Carnival from the great houses and put it on the streets, and to give it that wild, rich, fascinating character that was to make this Trinidad festival the unique occasion that it is today.

CHAPTER TWENTY

THE COMING OF ICE (1844)

On Tuesday, 17 September, 1844, readers of the Port-of-Spain Gazette may have been excited by the following advertisement appearing on page two of the four-page newspaper: "Ice! Ice! Ice! The Brig, New England, Captain McCurdy, has arrived from Boston with a cargo of ice."

This was the first time that a consignment of ice had arrived in Trinidad. The man to whom it was consigned was D.P. Cotton, who had for some time now been planning to bring ice to Trinidad. Only a month before, the editor of the Port-of-Spain Gazette had alluded to this matter, when he had written: "The long talked-of, often announced Ice House is at last in the course of erection. The first cargo of ice may be expected in about a week."

This Ice House was at the rear of Government House, which itself occupied part of the Treasury.

The editor's statement was made on 20 August, and it was just about a month later that the ice came. The well-to-do folks of Port-of-Spain seem to have got themselves all heated up—despite the fact that they were dealing with ice—and the Ice House appeared to be under constant siege.

On the day the ice arrived the proprietor of the Ice House, D.P. Cotton, put out a notice which said: "Ice will be sold in quantities not less than one pound, at five cents per pound, and in quantities not less than 100 pounds, at four cents per pound." Then he gave a bit of handy advice. "It is recommended," he said, "that all families using ice should furnish themselves with a good woolen blanket to convey the ice from the Ice House." And he inserted a little note: "A refrigerator is an indispensable item for economy."

So one can imagine the woolen blankets about Port-of-Spain used more for the covering of ice than for the covering of human beings. They were used both to take the ice from the Ice House and to preserve it, there being as yet no general sale of refrigerators to encourage the economy spoken of. This situation was not to last too long, for the manufacture of refrigerators in America was getting into full gear—so much so that by 1 October, Mr. Cotton could announce: "Received per Trinidad packet, and for sale, a few first and second size refrigerators." On the same occasion he advised people wishing ice on Sundays to present themselves before nine o'clock in the morning, as that was his closing hour on Sundays. He again reminded them about the qualities of a good woolen blanket—no doubt wishing they would preserve the ice they bought, and so bother him a little less.

Business seems to have been so good that the Ice House, which must have been a hurried, temporary structure, did not remain too long in the rear of Government House. Around the same time that those Government Offices moved from the Treasury Building to the new Government Offices on St. Vincent Street—a structure that was later to be called "The Red House"—the Ice House moved to other premises. It later occupied the south-eastern corner of Abercromby Street and Marine Square where the building remained until 1977.

From that occasion in 1844 the brigs with ice came frequently, bringing not only ice, but iced fruits and vegetables, and other such goods. And we know that ice remained a hot favourite—or rather, a cold favourite. Incidentally, ice cream came into its own at that time, and the Christmas of 1844 was the first time there was any advertisement

THE ICE HOUSE ON MARINE SQUARE WITH DELIVERY CARTS.

proclaiming ice cream in all flavours. Which is another way of saying that Christmas 1844 was the first Christmas that ice cream was eaten in Trinidad!

Naturally, D.P. Cotton flourished. He, too, became heated up, and flustered, for he could not handle the ice situation alone, and so he formed an Ice Company. The treasurer of the new Ice Company, far from being cool, called on shareholders to pay up their shares in full. Forthwith. For new and even more prosperous times were ahead. D.P. Cotton was now not only selling ice, and vegetables, and fruits on ice, and ice cream, and iced drinks, but he was putting meat on ice and fish on ice, and so doing all sorts of exciting things with ice, thus causing customers to throng the Ice House.

Even the well-to-do had to send or come often to the Ice House, for even if they had bought refrigerators, refrigerators then could not make ice, but only preserve it. Cotton's business boomed. The taste for ice, which soon took hold in Trinidad, was to become so ingrained that we can hardly imagine a time when people had to do without it.

So we remember the date, 17 September, 1844, when Captain McCurdy, in the brig "New England," brought ice to Trinidad for the first time.

CHAPTER TWENTY ONE

THE COMING OF THE FATEL ROZACK (ARRIVAL OF THE EAST INDIANS) (1845)

O n 30 May, 1845, a column in the Port-of-Spain Gazette
carried the following report: "We have much pleasure in
announcing the arrival of the long looked-for vessel, the
Fatel Rozack, 96 days from Calcutta and 41 days from the
Cape of Good Hope, with 217 on board, 'all in good order and
condition' as the bills of lading usually have it. There were five
deaths on board during the passage, but the general appearance of
the people is healthy. She was immediately boarded by the Harbour
Master, Health Officer, and the Agent-General for Immigrants."

The editorial ended: "The Fatel Rozack is a fine vessel of 415 tons
and manned by a crew of Lascars."

This was the moment of the arrival of the first East Indians to
come to Trinidad.

The Fatel Rozack was a comparatively small vessel—just 415 tons—
and there could not have been much comfort aboard, considering the
number of immigrants and the length of time the voyage took.

The majority of the immigrants who came on the Fatel Rozack
were very young people, for a look at their ages shows that 195 of them
were under 30. The oldest was a man called Ruchparr, who was 40. 23
were under 15, including 9 who were children under 10. Incidentally,
under the indentureship scheme, anyone over 10 was considered no

INDIAN IMMIGRANT

longer a child, and so had to take to the field. Of those under 10, one could have been considered a mere baby. She was Faizan, and was only 4 years of age.

While the Agent-General, the Honourable Henry Mitchell, was attending to the immigrants, the crowds of planters who had come to collect their quota of indentured workers as well as curious onlookers who had come down to the wharf to see what was going on, could not help but admire the Fatel Rozack. She lay at anchor at the lighthouse jetty, her mast tall and imposing, her white sails fluttering, probably being adjusted by the Lascars.

The governor in office was Sir Henry McLeod, and a promising event such as the arrival of indentured workers would hardly have found him sitting at his desk. In any case, at that time Government House was in the Treasury Building, so he would not have had far to walk, if he had chosen to go on foot.

Also there was the man who since the early days of Woodford had been advocating Indian indentured labour. Now, as a member of the Council of Government, he had worked hard to make this day come about. This was William Burnley. Burnley was not here just to see the Indians arrive. He owned large sugar plantations, among them the prominent Orange Grove estate, and he was here to collect his quota of workers too. Burnley had been allocated as many as 35 immigrants, based on the money he had put up. After the Agent-General had made

INDIAN IMMIGRANTS

the proper allocations, and after the health inspector had seen the newcomers, the immigrants landed, and although few would have been thinking of it, it was a moment of great significance for the future of Trinidad. No doubt, before these indentured immigrants got up onto horse-drawn carts, bound for their various estates, they must have looked around, having their first real glimpse of the country in which they found themselves.

They would have seen a very different waterfront from the one we have today. They would have seen the same light-house at the edge of the jetty, constructed in 1842, three years before the indentured immigrants came. They would have been taken out to South Quay, which was on the edge of the sea-side, and they might have noticed Fort San Andres, which is the site of a museum today, just at the corner of South Quay and the then spit of land leading to the jetty. They would have been taken out to King Street (today's Independence Square North), then an eastern turn on King Street, then after Duncan Street they would have crossed a precarious St. Ann's River (Dry River) bridge, and they would have been taken left along the St. Joseph Road, heading out of Port-of-Spain and for the estates.

CHAPTER TWENTYTWO

THE DIVISION OF THE ISLAND INTO COUNTIES AND WARDS (1849)

T he first time that counties and wards appeared in Trinidad, thus giving the island the first form of local government, was in September 1849, during the administration of Lord Harris.

When Harris arrived here in 1846 the interior of the island was virtually untouched despite more than three hundred years of Spanish possession, and indeed, after nearly half a century of British rule. The far flung coastal villages remained almost lost and forgotten, their planters being able to send produce to Port-of-Spain only when an occasional steamer passed by. There was a complete lack of road communication across the island, and the owners of estates that lay inland, and who, therefore, could not use the steamer service, were loudest in their cry for a solution to the problem.

Harris at once responded to the call. It was obvious to him that not only was there a need to help planters to get their produce out, but certain essential services had to be established. Schools had to be built, certainly roads had to be constructed, and some sort of island-wide control had to be effected. He also reasoned that a great deal of money had to be spent, and continually, in order to have these services, and of course Lord Harris knew who had to pay for all this!

Those who were crying out most, those who would use it most, and those who could afford, would have to pay for it. These were the planters, the owners of estates. Harris devised a plan whereby he would get landowners to assist in the development of the country, and at the same time set up a form of local management.

On 16 July, 1847—just one year after he arrived here—Lord Harris' plan to solve the development problem was passed in the Legislative Council, and the document carried the heading: "For the Division of the Colony of Trinidad into Divisions, Counties, Districts, and Wards". According to the plan, the Colony was first to be divided administratively into two divisions, each division comprising four counties, and each county in turn divided into two districts. The districts were then to be divided into wards.

For the division of the island into two parts Harris called for a line to be drawn from east to west, starting from Pointe-a-Pierre "and thence in a northeasterly direction along the heights of the Montserrat Hills to the head of the River Le Branche to the sea". All the areas north of this line was to be called the *Northern District*, and south of the line was to be called the *Southern District*.

Dealing with the Northern District the Ordinance said "the first (county) shall be called the *County of Saint George*, and shall comprise the islands of the Bocas, the island of Patos or Goose Island, and all such parts of the island of Trinidad as lie to the west of the River Aripo, along the eastern bank of the River Paria to its junction with the sea, and to the north of the River Caroni.

The second shall be called the *County of Saint David*, and shall comprise all such parts of the island as lie to the east of the River Aripo, and from a line drawn from the headwaters of the River Aripo, along the eastern bank of the River Paria to its junction with the sea, and to the north of the River Oropouche."

It said the third shall be called the *County of Caroni*, comprising such parts of the island as lie to the south of the Caroni River from the sea to its point of junction with the Aripo River, and to the north of a line drawn from Pointe-a-Pierre between the quarters of Savonetta and Pointe-a-Pierre and thence in a north-easterly direction along the heights of the Montserrat Hills until it meets a line drawn from the point of junction of the Caroni and Aripo rivers in a southerly direction to the Montserrat Hills, and to the west of such last-mentioned line.

Of the fourth and last county in the Northern District, it said: "And the fourth shall be called the *County of St. Andrew* and shall comprise all such parts of the island as lie to the east of such last mentioned line between the southern bank of the River Oropouche on the north and the southern bank of the River Le Branche.

The Ordinance decreed that the Southern District should also comprise four counties. It said that the first, *Victoria*, should lie within the following limits: "A line drawn from Pointe-a-Pierre between the quarters of Savonetta and Pointe-a-Pierre thence in a north-easterly direction to the Montserrat Hill till it meets the dividing line of the counties of Caroni and St. Andrew, thence in a southerly direction to the headwaters of the River Ortoire; and in a southwesterly direction to the eastern head of the Great Lagoon of Oropouche, and thence along the southern side of the Great Lagoon to the sea."

It named the second county as the *County of St. Patrick* and established its boundaries as the following: "All such parts of the island as lie to the south of the Great Lagoon of Oropouche and a line drawn from the eastern head of the said Lagoon to the headwaters of the River Guataro*, and to the west of a line drawn from the point where such last-mentioned line strikes the headwaters of the River Guataro, in a southerly direction till it meets the headwaters of the Moruga River, and thence along the eastern banks of the River Moruga to the sea."

The third county was to be *County Nariva* and its boundaries were simple: All the areas to the east of County Victoria, to the south of County St. Andrew, and to the north of the southern bank of the River Guataro.

Harris called the fourth county: *Mayaro*. Its boundaries were also easily defined: it was to comprise all such parts of the island as lie to the south of the southern banks of the River Guataro and to the east of the line herein before described as forming the eastern boundary of County St. Patrick.

---

* River Ortoire

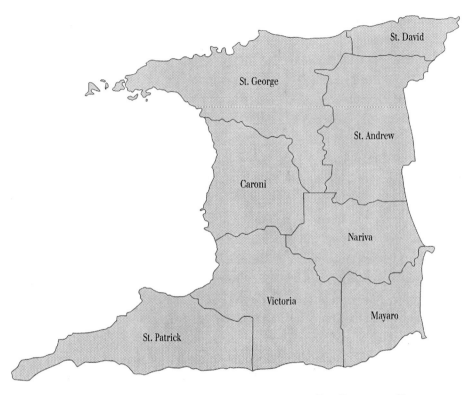

THE COUNTIES OF TRINIDAD

These were the eight counties, which in turn were to be divided into districts and wards. It will be noticed that Harris used the names of the patron saints of the British Isles for four of the counties: *St. George* (Patron Saint of England), *St. Andrew* (Patron Saint of Scotland), *St. David* (Patron Saint of Wales), and *St. Patrick* (Patron Saint of Ireland). For the large and important County of Victoria, embracing the Naparimas, he commemorated the young English Queen Victoria.

The three remaining counties were confirmed in Amerindian names: *Caroni*, on the west, was named after the river the Amerindians called by that name. *Nariva* on the east was also a tribute to the Amerindians, and *Mayaro* had an old Arawak settlement of the same name.

CHAPTER TWENTYTHREE

THE FIRST PUBLIC LIBRARY IN TRINIDAD (1851)

O n 1 February, 1851, Governor Lord Harris put before the Council of Government an Ordinance of which the following is the first clause: "Whereas it is expedient to promote the establishment of a Public Library in the Town of Port-of-Spain for the instruction and amusement of the inhabitants thereof, be it enacted by His Excellency the Governor, by and with the consent of the Council of Government, that there shall be paid from the Colonial Treasury towards the maintenance of a Public Library in the Town of Port-of-Spain the yearly sum of three hundred pounds."

Even in 1851, three hundred pounds sterling ($1,440.00) was not a great deal for the government to put out for an institution of refinement, although many might have complained that a library was meant to serve the leisured class. If that was so, then Harris could have retorted that the library was meant to be public, and therefore in the service of all.

In any event, Harris was presenting the Ordinance to the Council of Government, and the Ordinance was approved and duly passed into law on Friday, 7 February, 1851.

While the government was looking about for a place to house the library, a notice appearing in the newspapers called upon the Secretary/Librarian to attend at the Red House daily for the purpose of dealing with correspondence and other matters relating to the setting up of the library. For the time being, the office was to be the vacant judge's chamber, and the hours were to be 10 a.m. to 1 p.m. and from 2 p.m. to 6 p.m.

So Harris was very serious about the library, and he had the trait of following up a matter to the end once it was begun. As much as he esteemed the members of his Council of Government, he did not want to entrust the running of the institution to them, and so he called together some of the most distinguished men in Port-of-Spain and formed a Library Committee. Since the Treasury was finding the money to run the library, he could not entirely exclude members of his government—especially so as there had to be a link between the government and the public. He kept this in mind when he announced the names of the members of the first Library Committee. This comprised the Chief Justice John Knox; the Attorney-General Charles Warner; a member of his Council of Government, John Losh; then there was the representative of the Roman Catholics, Archbishop Patrick Smith; representing the Anglicans was Archdeacon George Cummings, and there was Augustin Thoulouis, a well-known person of refinement.

Harris invited the Port-of-Spain Town Council to name two representatives. The Town Council named Louis de Verteuil, who was at the time Chairman of the Town Council (and soon to become the first Mayor of Port-of-Spain), and with him it named Doctor Court.

Harris had envisaged the library as being free, but because of factors relating to its upkeep and its stocking of books it became a subscriber's library. In fact it became free only in 1951. There was no question of it being a lending library - this was to come much later.

After Harris's Library Ordinance was passed on 7 February, 1851, the matter of setting up the library was never allowed to flag, and in fact, on 27 May that year one could read the following advertisement: "Notice is hereby given that the reading rooms of the library will be opened to the public on Monday next, the 2nd of June. Until arrangements can be made for lighting the rooms the reading rooms will be opened from 7 a.m. to 10 a.m. and from 11 a.m. to 6 p.m."

This notice was signed by J. Danglade, the first Secretary/Librarian.

THE LIBRARY ON KNOX STREET WITH OLD TOWN HALL BUILDING IN THE DISTANCE.

The reading rooms stayed in the Government Building for some years, but to find the Public Library in the 1880s one would have had to go to Chacón Street. The library remained at Chacón Street to see the century close. By then, plans were well advanced to move from the congested Chacón Street quarters, and everybody must have been elated because a classical and ornate library building was going up on the eastern corner of Pembroke and Knox Streets. This building was nearly ready in 1901 (the date it bears on its front facade) but was completed in early 1902. The date was 21 March, 1902, when the library was installed in its new home.

It is interesting that 51 years after the library was established it moved to this site, which 51 years before (1800) was the site of the house of Trinidad's first Governor, Sir Thomas Picton. In fact the old building seems to have been demolished to make way for the library.

The date to remember is Friday, 7 February, 1851, when it all began, for it was the day when Lord Harris got approval for his Ordinance—Ordinance 2 of 1851, which was headed: "An Ordinance for the establishment of a public library in the Town of Port-of-Spain."

CHAPTER TWENTYFOUR

THE FIRST WATER SYSTEM IN TRINIDAD (1851)

I n Port-of-Spain the age of water-wells seemed to be coming to a close when in 1841 a water company was formed with the intention of bringing water into the town in pipes. Early in 1841, the company declared its aim of bringing water from the St. Ann's and Maraval rivers right into the centre of Port-of-Spain, supplying a number of streets from the Queen's Park (the Queen's Park Savannah today) to the wharf.

It was the first time that people in Trinidad were hearing of such new-fangled ideas as taking water through pipes to their own houses — although, of course, this was already common in many cities of the world. Indeed right here, in 1820, Governor Ralph Woodford had done this: he had piped water from the St. Ann's River to his residence, St. Ann's Cottage. (The site of St. Ann's Cottage is occupied today by the President's House, which was formerly the Governor's residence, built in 1875.)

In 1841, in which period Woodford's Cottage was occupied by Governor Sir Henry McLeod, the Water Company was the focus of attention, promising, as it did, a new era for Port-of-Spain. In trying to realise its plans, it could not really prevail against some determined landowners who were in its proposed route. Some of the landowners concerned refused to allow access through their property to the banks of the rivers mentioned. A few were willing to sell the necessary land but the prices they were quoting seemed totally unrealistic to the Water Company. After wrangles and a great number of legal tussles, and after a frightening amount of useless expenditure, the Water Company could do nothing but withdraw.

The Water Company was in the process of withdrawal when Governor Lord Harris came here in 1845. The town, so insanitary, was in such a dire need of water that Harris could not look upon this failure lightly. From the point of view of public health, this was one of the worst periods for the town, which was now nothing but a collection of shacks, frequently swept by disease, most of which resulted from the pollution of its wells. For those who could see into the future, this period heralded the worst health scourge Port-of-Spain was ever to know—the cholera epidemic of 1854.

So Harris, on his advent in 1845, made it clear to the Legislative Council that something had to be done in respect of a water system. He got the government to agree to buy up the pipes and other materials that the Water Company had already assembled, and he proceeded to work on an Ordinance providing for the very legislation that the Water Company had sought—legislation affecting access.

But with several other pressing projects that Harris was undertaking, the months slipped by, and it was not until the year 1850 that a positive step was taken towards establishing a water system. At a meeting of the Legislative Council on 5 October, 1850, Harris announced he was ready for action on the question of water.

He went so far as to take money out of a sum voted to complete the Government Offices—the building which later became the Red House—helping himself to the equivalent of $40,000. To this, he pressed the Port-of-Spain Town Council to add $30,000. Incidentally, members of the Council of Government felt that the Town Council should have borne the entire burden, and there were those, like William Burnley, who felt that if the Town Council failed to do that, then government should lay down the system alone.

The Water Company, on its withdrawal, had already dug a reservoir in the Queen's Park—today the Hollows mark that spot—and it had already run water from the St. Ann's River to it, through the

MARAVAL RESERVOIR

Botanic Gardens, by means of a channel later called the Nutmeg Ravine. That supply alone was inadequate, however, and a report of 1850, hostile to Harris, said: "It must be generally known that the town is supplied with water only by that meagre conduit which starts from the digue and dies away impotently at Marine Square."

The digue, or dam, was on the St. Ann's River, but it was the Maraval river that was the powerful source, and Harris, after approaching the stubborn landowners with courtesy, and receiving the same blunt refusal as the Water Company before him, decided that enough was enough. A Water Ordinance which he drafted and which gained the approval of the Legislative Council in November 1851 said in part: "And be it enacted ... that it shall be lawful that the Superintendent of Public Works and his workmen shall pass on lands of Eliza Piggot La Coste, Jean de Boissiere and Henry Boissiere; the Rookery, of Henry Fuller; lands of Fritz and William Urich; and on the St. Clair Estate, then across Circular Road, and any other land whatsoever, along the way, in line with a strip thirty feet wide for sinking and laying the pipes."

And it was by that means that the first system of pipe-borne water was established in Trinidad. The inception and the dream was in 1841 when the Water Company was formed but it was from November 1851 that work could start in earnest in building such a system in Port-of-Spain.

CHAPTER TwentyFive

THE FIRST SYSTEM OF PRIMARY SCHOOLS (1851)

THE FIRST SYSTEM OF PRIMARY SCHOOLS (1851)

The first system of primary education in Trinidad emerged in 1851, when Lord Harris, having established the wards, called on each warden to open at least one school.

Lord Harris felt strongly about the fact that, save the church schools, the children of the masses had no school to go to. He was very much alert to the fact that the main objective of the church schools was to teach religion, a matter which kept away children who were not of the persuasion. As a result Harris had said: "If the schools are to be used by all, the instruction afforded should be such as all will readily accept."

But Harris knew that this was not going to be so, and the 12th rule of his resolution on the setting up of schools states: "That the instruction to be given at the training and primary schools be secular, and without direct religious or doctrinal teaching."

The governor had moved quickly on this matter of primary education in Trinidad. Having arrived in April 1845, he took up the issue on 1 February, 1847. Addressing the Legislative Council on that date, he had said: "The Governor proposes that one, or if necessary, two or more primary schools should be established in each ward ... which schools should be open to the children of all inhabitants."

Anticipating the opposition of the planters to this measure he declared: "There is every reason to believe that an educated population is a more moral one than an uneducated population, and that the expenses of Government are materially diminished in those departments which are made necessary in order to repress the errors, the vices, the crimes, which ignorance, more than anything else, entails on society."

He had said this in 1846, before the wards were established, and so the system could not be introduced because Harris was depending on money from ward rates to run the primary schools. Counties and wards were not finally established until 1849, and two years later Harris felt himself ready. In a resolution of 19 April, 1851, Harris made some major proposals on the issue. He proposed that a Board of Education be formed, that an Inspector of Schools be appointed, that a training school for teachers be started, and that ward schools be established at once. On the last proposal his words were: "That there be at once established in each ward of the colony as many schools and at such places as are most suitable for the convenience of the population as may be determined by the warden of the ward and approved by the Governor."

The first ward schools were established in districts around Port-of-Spain, such as Maraval, Diego Martin, San Juan, Santa Cruz—and surprisingly enough one was established as far away as Mayaro.

To a great extent these schools replaced or competed with the church schools, and so with the clergy seeing their influence diminished, they whipped up heated opposition to Harris' policies. The 12th clause, which opposed religious instruction, was cited to declare Harris an ungodly and evil man. They made it appear that it was not simply a case of Harris against the clergy, but Harris against God. In any case, teachers openly flouted the rule on religious instruction.

Harris left here as governor in 1854, but the primary school system remained as one of the key issues. In 1869, the Secretary of State for the Colonies sent an Irishman, Patrick Keenan, to observe and report on the system of primary education in Trinidad. As a whole, Keenan found the schools very badly run. There were 30 ward schools already established, and Keenan felt that they were not worth the public money spent on them.

Keenan, carrying out the most meticulous enquiry, found that Harris' rule about no religion in classes was openly flouted. He himself was a devout Catholic and felt this rule should be changed. He had a high esteem for priests, and he felt that discipline, which was sadly lacking among the teachers, could be best imposed by priests. As to the wardens, who were the school managers, he described them as completely incapable. They did not even seem interested in the schools, and many of the schools lacked such fundamental necessities as desks, blackboards, and even clocks to tell the time. What Keenan recommended in the end could be considered quite a blow to Harris' scheme. In his report to the Secretary of State for the Colonies, Earl Granville, he said: "Your Lordship will, I am sure, be prepared to hear that I most urgently recommend a radical change in the present system ... I propose that the management of each ward school should be invested in a clergyman of the same religion as the majority of the pupils."

He also recommended that schools with Roman Catholic majorities—there were 20 such schools—be handed over to the Roman Catholic church. He named eight schools with Anglican majorities and asked that they be handed over to the Anglican church.

Keenan's report was largely accepted, but Harris' idea prevailed in the end. The schools in question were handed over to the church, but this made it quite clear that the government should set up and run its own schools—government schools.

But whether religion was the issue or not, Harris' dream was well on the way to coming true. He had ended his resolution of 19 April 1851, with the words: "I am desirous that the means and opportunities for obtaining instruction should be afforded to every child in this island."

And so 19 April, 1851, is a memorable date: it was the first time that a system of education for the children of the masses was started in Trinidad.

CHAPTER TWENTY SIX

THE FIRST INLAND POSTAL SERVICE (1851)

S o far as the establishment of an inland postal service is concerned, we have to look back at the date 14 August, 1851. Previous to that date, we find that although it was possible to communicate with a friend by letter in almost any part of the world, it would have been impossible to do the same if one lived in Trinidad.

There was no such thing as an inland postal service here. Indeed, no such thing existed in any of the colonial territories, and it was only in the previous year, 1850, that the British Parliament passed an Act enabling Colonial Legislatures to establish inland posts. No sooner had Queen Victoria signed this Act in September 1850, that plans were put in motion here to introduce an Ordinance for such a service. The result was that on the historic morning of 14 August, 1851, two mounted policemen rode off from the General Post Office on Frederick Street, bringing into being the first inland postal service in Trinidad. Mr. James O'Brien was the first postmaster, and the General Post Office was the police station.

The 14 August, 1851, was a Thursday, and it might seem strange that a service was started on this day of the week instead of on a Monday, for instance. However, the people of the island could have borne no grudge against the governor, who was Lord Harris, if he chose to mark his birthday with this historic event. At any rate he deserved it, for despite the busy early months about which we shall read in this section of the work, he had turned his attention to this with such enthusiasm that by April he was able to introduce, as well as proclaim, Ordinance 6 of 1851, setting up an inland postal service for Trinidad.

Anyway, the policemen turned their horses down Frederick Street towards the waterfront and it appears they went to the wharf first to deliver to the coastal steamer "Lady McLeod" the mails for the southern part of the island.

This first postal service linked Port-of-Spain with twenty districts in Trinidad. These districts were: Chacachacare, Monos, Carenage and Diego Martin—all in the northwestern region; Santa Cruz, San Juan, St. Joseph, Arima and Arouca—crucial centres, all relatively nearby; Chaguanas, Couva, San Fernando, Savana Grande, Oropouche, La Brea and Cedros—areas lying to the west and to the south; Turure, Manzanilla and Nariva—remote eastern settlements lying inland; and the key district, Mayaro, on the south-east coast.

In this era of the mid-nineteenth century, when there was a dire lack of good roads in Trinidad, most of the mail had to go by sea. Indeed, only seven of the twenty districts could be reached without crossing water—these being the districts of Santa Cruz, Carenage, Diego Martin, San Juan, St. Joseph, Arima, and Arouca.

Yet Diego Martin and Carenage began with a service that was only twice-weekly: Mondays and Fridays. The rest of these accessible places, namely: Santa Cruz, San Juan, St. Joseph, Arouca, and Arima, saw the postman every day, except on Sundays.

In the case of the districts reached by water, Chaguanas received mails on Tuesdays, Thursdays, and Saturdays. At the same time, districts as far distant as Couva, San Fernando, Savana Grande, and Oropouche, received mails five days a week: from Monday to Saturday, omitting Friday.

And how fared the remote eastern districts of Turure, Nariva, Manzanilla, and Mayaro? Surprisingly, not worse than the gulf coast

ONE OF THE VERY RARE POSTAL STAMPS OF THE WORLD: THE BLUE LADY MCLEOD
USED EXCLUSIVELY TO TRANSPORT MAIL ON THE STEAMER OF THE SAME NAME

villages of La Brea and Cedros. And indeed not worse than the
relatively nearby islets of Monos and Chacachacare. All these places
received their letters once a week—the east coast districts on Mondays,
and the rest on Saturdays.

There was no such thing as postmen when the service first started,
and to quote Lord Harris, "I never contemplated the luxury." But the
problem of delivery was in the country areas. In the towns it was easy
to have the policemen deliver the letters.

Postmen were not introduced until 1860, and the first postman's
knock was on Wednesday, 26 September, 1860. The date to bear in
mind is 14 August, 1851, when at eight o'clock in the morning two
policemen on horseback galloped from the police station on Frederick
Street to establish the first inland postal service in Trinidad.

CHAPTER TWENTY SEVEN

THE FIRST RAILWAY IN TRINIDAD (1859)

T he first railway to be established in Trinidad was the Cipero Tramroad, a planters' line which plied between what is now Princes Town and the wharf at San Fernando. (Princes Town was then known as Mission, or to give it full title: The Mission of Savana Grande.)

The Cipero Tramway was opened on Saturday, 5 March, 1859, with great pomp and jubilation, for with it a new age had stepped in for the sugarplanters of the Naparimas. The chief force behind the tramway was a wealthy sugar planter of the region, William Eccles, whose initial plan was to go much beyond the construction of the tramway. He established the line primarily to bring produce from the remote estates in the Naparimas out to the San Fernando wharf, and to the waiting ships and sloops.

In preparation for the project, Eccles had formed a company called the Naparima Harbour, Land, and Tramroad Company, and so his aim was not just to transport sugarcane, but to develop the whole of that strip of country, even exploring the source of the River Ortoire, which was somewhat near to Mission, and in so doing, to use the words of the company, "Opening up the country from sea to sea."

Not too long after the inauguration of the tramway, which, of course, was strictly for the transport of produce, there was a great demand for the transport of workers from one estate to the other along the line. It was a demand that seemed so reasonable that the tramway authorities found it difficult to ignore it. Also, a number of important people who normally rode to and from these centres on horseback would have been happy to avoid the rigours of such travel and ride the tramway. Because of these demands, the owners of the tramway provided convenience for a few passengers, thus starting the tramway's first passenger service. Apart from this, there had always been the need to take messages to and from Mission, and it had not always been convenient to send someone. Again, as a result of pressure, not only by businessmen but by the San Fernando public, the Cipero Tramroad started, in 1866, the first postal service between San Fernando and Mission. At the start of the service the mail van left Harris Promenade on Mondays and Wednesdays.

The tram road took its name from the Cipero River, which had its source in the vicinity of the tram road terminus and wound through many of the sugar estates on its route, providing the main shipping place for sugar in San Fernando of that period. An *embarcadere* (an improvised wharf) was established at that point, and today the place is still known as Embarcadere. At the tramline's terminus in today's Princes Town, two places commemorate the Cipero Tramroad—Tramline Street, and Tramway Road.

From the terminus, the trams, which at first were carriages drawn by horses or mules, passed through the village of Sainte Madeleine, which in later years was to have the largest sugar factory in the British West Indies. This factory, the famous *Usine*, was erected by the Colonial Company in 1872.

But we are back at the start of the Cipero Tramroad. After leaving the Naparima estates, it entered San Fernando on the southern side, at a point then called the Cipero Cross because here the road leading southwards from San Fernando crossed the Cipero River near its mouth. Here soon became a railway crossing, which was called Cross Crossing. After leaving canes at the *embarcadere*, the Cipero tram

An early Locomotive.

came through a stretch that is today Lady Hailes Avenue, then across what later became known as Broadway (now Independence Avenue). In the very early days, the Cipero Tramroad had its final station (in fact, its starting point) on Harris Promenade.

But in 1867, the Cipero Tramroad achieved a noteworthy objective: rails were laid from Harris Promenade to the San Fernando wharf. A cutting was made beside Chancery Lane, but this cutting posed the greatest difficulty and it was years before it came into use. With Chancery Lane on the one hand and the little hospital buildings on the other, it was plagued by landslides, the subject of numerous complaints.

When the noted English writer Charles Kingsley came to San Fernando at the beginning of 1870, he had to come up to Harris Promenade to catch the tramway, which took him to the village of Mission. He later wrote about the tramway and about the trip in his book "At Last, A Christmas in the West Indies." At the time that he came, the tramroad already had a reliable and frequent passenger service. Two vans were in operation: one left San Fernando at 7.30 every morning and again in the early afternoon, and the other one left Mission at the same times, coming the other way. The vans stopped at Victoria Village, Sainte Madeleine, and Malgretout. Passengers making the journey paid 36 cents.

The Cipero Tramroad was a great success and lasted up to the 1920s, when it was absorbed into the Trinidad Government Railway.

OIL PIONEERS WALTER DARWENT,
RANDOLPH RUST AND JOHN LEE LUM.

CHAPTER TwentyEight

THE FIRST OIL WELL DRILLED IN TRINIDAD (1867)

THE FIRST OIL WELL IN TRINIDAD (1867)

The first oil well in Trinidad was drilled by the English engineer Walter Darwent, who at the time lived in San Fernando. Darwent, who had been reacting to a survey report by two geologists, was certain that he could find oil.

The two geologists were Wall and Sawkins, and they came here in 1860. The world had just then been in the process of discovering the great use of petroleum as a fuel, and Wall and Sawkins, observing the curious asphalt deposit at La Brea, decided to do a thorough geological survey of southern Trinidad. They appreciated the close connection between petroleum and asphalt. Wall and Sawkins carried out their extensive investigation in 1860 and published valuable information which left no doubt that petroleum could be extracted from various areas of the country.

Darwent was the first prospector to come in their wake. In the year 1867, Darwent, using a primitive wooden derrick in the forests of Aripero, South Trinidad, started his drilling operation. He had only gone down to a depth of 200 feet when he struck a bed of oil.

However, with his primitive equipment, Darwent had taken some time to reach this depth, and the operation proved very costly. The crucial part of the operation—getting the oil out of the earth— seemed beyond him. So after seeing his dream half-fulfilled, the brave oil pioneer had to give up. Also, in the unhealthy forests of Aripero he must have contracted illness of some sort, for soon afterwards he died.

(Incidentally, Darwent's effort was not only the first in Trinidad but the first in the western world, for it was not until 1868 that Drake drilled the first American oil well.)

Walter Darwent's achievement at Aripero stirred the imagination to such an extent that when the famous English writer, Charles Kingsley, came here during the Christmastide of 1869/1870, he was taken to see Darwent's well. Kingsley, a Canon of the Anglican Church, was not at all sympathetic to Darwent's effort, looking upon it as an interference in God's work. It was only two years since Darwent had drilled the well, and the open cavern was still fresh amidst the forest trees. Kingsley described it as a sore in the lush scenery. He looked at the black petroleum sputtered about the well, the substance that could not be got out in quantities, and he rejoiced, saying that that should teach Man to mind his own business.

For more than 20 years afterwards, the prospectors appeared to be minding their own business—although, in fact, a feverish search had been going on under-cover. In 1870, a forest-ranger found seepages of oil in the Guayaguayare forest, and this intensified the search in that area. John Lee Lum, a merchant in the area, became extremely eager, and possibly through him the Port-of-Spain merchant, Randolph Rust, came on the scene. It was not until the year 1893 that a decisive phase was reached in Trinidad oil exploration. Rust, exploring in the Guayaguayare area, came upon oil. Wiser than Darwent, he did not attempt to drill without solid financial backing, for it proved a costly enterprise. Rust, who was of Canadian origin, sought this financial backing for eight years, until he finally persuaded a Canadian whiskey company to join with him in the oil enterprise. Together they formed a company called "The Oil Exploration Syndicate of Canada". After drilling moderately successful wells at Guayaguayare, the costliness of the project caused the Oil Exploration Syndicate of Canada to pull out, but by that time it had done enough to convince oil explorers that there was a great deal of oil in the Guayaguayare area, and it had provided an incentive for oil exploration elsewhere. Rust continued

JOHN LEE LUM AT THE FIRST PRODUCING OIL WELL IN SOUTHERN TRINIDAD.

and the year 1902 marked his great find. By the next decade another company, Trinidad Leaseholds Limited, encountered gushing oil near La Brea, in the area known as Forest Reserve. Its well, "Helena," drilled in 1914, is active even today. The World War, which began in 1914, generated the Trinidad Government's interest in oil, and there was a flurry of activity in that sector. Trinidad exported oil for the first time.

The 1920s saw about a dozen concerns drilling for oil in Trinidad and by the mid-1930s, oil had already become the backbone of the economy.

Notwithstanding that, by the 1960s the high point of Trinidad oil production was past—just about 100 years after Walter Darwent drilled the first well—it is good to look back on those early years, especially at that wooden derrick at Aripero with the oil-spattered hole beneath it, and maybe one could be glad that, contrary to Kingsley's advice, Man did not "mind his own business."

TWENTYNINE
CHAPTER

THE FIRST PASSENGER RAILWAY IN TRINIDAD (1876)

I t was the year 1846 that marked the start of the railway story in Trinidad and therefore the start of our first such public transport system.

But it took many decades, of course, for this transport system to appear. What happened in 1846 was the formation of a Trinidad Railway Company, and this Company proceeded to survey the length and breadth of this country with the intention of establishing a railway system. In the end, it could not go ahead with plans because of failure to raise the required finance. The company continued in existence and through the ensuing years the idea was kept very much alive. In 1859 William Eccles brought into being a successful tramroad company in the south, and this may have given new hope to the still surviving Trinidad Railway Company. In 1873, this company carried out another extensive survey of the country, and this time finance was forthcoming, for they began laying down the railway lines.

This work started on South Quay, Port-of-Spain, just north of the lighthouse jetty, and the first section was laid down to San Juan. From San Juan station trial runs began. A long row of wooden buildings was erected on South Quay, where the work had started, and this was to be the first railway station.

The work of laying down the lines progressed from San Juan to St. Joseph, but it was Arima that was the objective. Great preparation was made, a station was built at Arima, and the line finally reached it. And it was on Santa Rosa Day, Thursday, 31 August, 1876, that the train set out for Arima to start the first railway service in Trinidad. Government officials mingled with the hundreds of passengers who made the first trip. A reporter from the Port-of-Spain Gazette was amongst these passengers too, and he wrote: "The trains were run up, and then down, and the greatest regularity was observed. The three last trains were late, but that was only to be expected. Altogether, the Government and the railway officials are to be congratulated on the success of the opening."

The entire population was jubilant about the coming of the railway, for in 1876 there were few proper roads for the horses and buggies and donkeycarts to travel along, and even so, during the rainy season those earthen roads were often impassable. Rail offered not only speed but the only means of all weather travel. There was a clamour for the extension of the railway, especially so among the sugar planters of the west coast. So the southern line was started almost immediately, and by the beginning of 1880, the line to Couva was almost ready. Or maybe it was hurriedly made so, for the governor of the day, Sir Henry Irving, had two very important visitors he wanted to take on the railway.

The first run on that line was on 16 January, 1880, and the next issue of the Port-of-Spain Gazette said: "On Monday the good people of Couva were treated to a royal visit. At about eleven o'clock in the forenoon, a train arrived at the railway station there, bearing His Excellency the Governor Sir Henry Irving ... and their Royal Highnesses Prince Albert Victor and Prince George."

These were the sons of King Edward VII, and the grandsons of Queen Victoria. Albert Victor was 16 at the time. His brother, Prince George, who was 15, later became King George V. The Couva line was opened to the public soon afterwards.

The railway continued to press southwards, and in April 1882 it reached San Fernando. The line was opened on April 16 that year. In 1884 a service from San Fernando to Princes Town was inaugurated.

(Incidentally, the village of Mission was named Princes Town on the occasion of the princes' visit to that village in 1880.)

OPENING OF THE RAILWAY STATION.

The line to Arima was doing exceptionally well and had given cocoa a great boost. The Sangre Grande cocoa planters began to cry out for an extension of the service and the line was extended to Guanapo in 1896, then on to Sangre Grande in 1897. The formal opening of the Sangre Grande line was on the 1st of September that year.

In 1898 the railway line branched off from the Cunupia Farm, a point on the southern line, and ran through the Caparo Valley to Tabaquite. The junction made at the Cunupia Farm became known as Jerningham Junction, after the governor of the time, Sir Hubert Jerningham.

The railway reaching the cocoa lands at Tabaquite was not the end of the matter. Sugar and cocoa had been served, but what about oil? In 1913, when oil earnestly began to flow, the San Fernando line was extended through the oil regions to Siparia. There were further outcries from the cocoa planters in the deep Caparo Valley, and the year 1914 saw the railway being extended to Rio Claro.

And this was to be the extent of the Trinidad Government Railway. The system lasted until the 1960s when, for many reasons, the system was scrapped. The last section of the line went out in 1968. The important date to remember is 31 August, 1876, the day that saw the running of the first passenger train in Trinidad.

CHAPTER THIRTY

THE FIRST TRAMS (1883)

T he first tramcar service in Trinidad started on the afternoon of Thursday, 27 December, 1883, when a cheering holiday crowd, gathered in front of the railway station on South Quay, saw a new era in transport come in.

The directors of the tramway service must have felt worried and nervous when the service was about to start, for none knew what would happen on these first trips. The trams were carriages drawn by mules, stubborn mules, and before the appointed day, the tramway company had had the mules go through the most careful practice in preparation. The company would have allowed even more time for this preparation, but, owing to one of the clauses in their lease, they had to start before 1883 ended, and so they chose one of the latest days possible, Thursday, 27 December. The mules were put into harness on that day, amid misgivings, but luckily, everything turned out well. In fact, one of the reporters even spoke of the performance of the mules as being "in excellent style".

But it was the next day that the service was put to the test. This was not due to the performance of the mules—which seemed to be managing—but to the demand for transport on that day. For that occasion, Friday, 28 December, was the first day of the Christmas Race Meeting at the Queen's Park Savannah. The great crowds who came to

Port-of-Spain by train no longer wanted to walk up to the Queen's Park Savannah but had to be taken there "in excellent style" too, by the mule trams. Especially so as the tramway company had been advertising the service for weeks before. On that day, the 28th, the crowds were so great that the four trams the company was using could hardly cope. So some would have certainly been disappointed, and would have had to walk. These must have missed a treat, seeing the horse "Wyanoke" win the Governor's Cup. One consolation was that the governor himself, Sir Sanford Freeling, was not there—and this was a subject of much censure.

The next day must have been an even more difficult day for race-goers, for it was a rainy Saturday, and a Saturday with even more people in town, being the New Year weekend, as well as a weekend of exciting prospects at the races. So with only four trams plying, many more people would have had to walk to the Queen's Park Savannah. And so many would have missed seeing the horse "Ruth Howard" dominate the day's racing. Wyanoke seemed to have avoided Ruth Howard, and many claimed that she was being hidden from this horse.

But horses came and went and observers of the scene must have been talking of the trams, a new feature in Port-of-Spain life. They must have appreciated it as the first system of public transport in the town. How would they have described this new vehicle?

These trams were each drawn by two mules. The mules were of an especially sturdy breed, imported from the United States. The trams were open carriages, with a footboard running along each side, and each had six rows. They ran on rails.

Although the trams were open, there were screens to be let down in case of rainy weather, and they must have come in handy on that Saturday of blustery rain. However, the driver was not screened. He had his seat at the front, outside of the tram, for he was of course in control of the horses.

The time-table of the tram service on that occasion was the following:

- From the railway station to St. Ann's Road (via Frederick Street) every 20 minutes.

MULE TRAM

- From the railway station to St. Ann's Road (via St. Vincent Street) every 40 minutes.
- To Newtown (via Frederick Street) every 40 minutes.
- To Newtown (via St. Vincent Street and Tranquillity) every 20 minutes.
- The trams for Newtown and Tranquillity were painted red, and those for St. Ann's Road were painted blue.

The first directors of the tramway company were: H. Hoffman, J. Bell-Smythe, H.E. Rapsey, and C.F. Stollmeyer.

CHAPTER THIRTY ONE

THE FIRST TIME THE TELEPHONE RANG (1885)

T he first time the telephone rang in Trinidad was not in the year the service was truly established.

The first time the telephone service could be said to have been established in Trinidad was on the 15 January, 1885, when the first telephone exchange was opened in Port-of-Spain. There had been serious, though not wholly successful attempts to establish a telephone service here since 1883. Wires were strung, telephones were connected, and a few of the pieces of equipment actually worked. In 1884 quite a few business places seemed to be on the telephone. Yet these first few attempts were disorganised, and one could not speak in terms of a "telephone system".

They drew widespread attention and comment because of the very uniqueness of the telephone. It was the first time in this country one could converse with anybody who was out of normal earshot. It was only when a telephone exchange was opened on 15 January, 1885, that a telephone system was established, notwithstanding that on Old Year's Day, 1883, the *New Era* newspaper commented: "The introduction and establishing of the telephone communications is another thing in connection with advances ... which must be noted as among the notable occurrences of 1883."

The man who started a telephone system here in January 1885 was Adelbert W. Gray, who had come to Trinidad in 1883 as an agent of the Tropical American Telephone Company Limited. Mr. Gray had come to set up a telephone system here, and he let the commercial sector know this, but no sooner had he begun work, planting poles and installing equipment, than he ran into trouble with the Tropical American Company. Apparently there was some difficulty about payments made to him and he paid himself out of the company's funds. This seemed fair enough, but when he returned to New York for instructions, they had him arrested for embezzlement. The court cleared him, and Mr. Gray, bitter with the company, but wanting to keep his promises to the commercial sector here, decided to come back to Trinidad to continue his work on the setting up of a telephone system. Only that this time he was no longer Mr. Gray of the Tropical American Company. Now he was working for himself. He discarded the equipment of his former company and out of his own resources brought in new equipment to do his work.

Gray seemed to have made many close friends here, and one of his closest and most loyal friends was the Editor of the *New Era* newspaper, Joseph Lewis. Shortly before Gray had been cleared of the embezzlement charge and, in fact, even before he had returned to Trinidad, Lewis had notified the public through his newspaper: "It is confidently expected that the new telephone exchange will be in operation next January."

Gray arrived back in Trinidad in November 1884 and at once published the following: "I, the undersigned, beg most respectfully to notify the public in general that I am now prepared to receive further orders for subscribers to my telephone exchange, which is to be opened in January next."

In that same notice he published his rates of rental, which stated: "For business houses within one mile of the exchange, $4 per month, payable in advance. For residences of business subscribers within city limits $3 per month, payable in advance. For residences of non-business subscribers within city limits, $3.50 per month, payable in advance." He advised that special arrangements would be made for

THE NOVELTY OF THE TELEPHONE MADE IT A POPULAR PROP TO PHOTOGRAPHERS.

rates of construction and rentals beyond the city limits. Shortly after this announcement, it was noticed that he had connected up the whole of the commercial sector of Port-of-Spain.

Gray's exchange was situated at numbers 3 and 4 Almond Walk, a street which is known as Broadway today. His exchange received overwhelming requests for subscribers, and he at once saw that he would not be able to cope, and that the enterprise had to be extended and would be very much bigger than he had foreseen. So what did he do? To take some of the burden off his shoulders he decided to form a company, and invited shares. The company was formed on Thursday, 5 March, 1885, and at that point there were 200 subscribers. hat number was going to be the limit for the time being. The company was called the Trinidad Telephone Company Limited. It was launched with eight people, collectively holding 335 shares.

Not long afterwards one saw the following notice in the newspapers: "I hereby notify the public that my telephone exchange has been opened and working since January 15. I have to apologise to such of my subscribers as are somewhat distant from the exchange for the unavoidable delay in putting in their telephones, but the work is being rapidly pushed on, and within a very few days I hope to have my subscribers, even in the most distant parts of the town, connected."

And so 15 January, 1885, is the date one can look back upon to record the establishment of a telephone service in Trinidad.

ThirtyTwo
CHAPTER
The First Time the Issue of a Franchise was Raised (1888)

I t was in the year 1887 that Reverend Robert Andrews went to San Fernando to what was called "patriotic celebrations" and returned with what some would have called "unpatriotic" thoughts stirring inside him.

The celebrations, which took place in June 1887, were in commemoration of the Golden Jubilee of Queen Victoria. It was 50 years since she had acceded to the British throne.

Reverend Andrews lived at Fifth Company Village, on the Moruga Road, and a settlement more neglected by the authorities would have been hard to find. The villagers of Fifth Company lacked all the normal amenities, but the shortcoming they felt most was the lack of good roads.

Reverend Andrews saw the wild hysteria in San Fernando on the occasion of Victoria's jubilee; he heard the church-bells tolling, saw the town festooned with flags and buntings, knew of the banquets of the rich and dinners for the poor, and heard patriotic speeches and declarations. His conclusion was that there was overwhelming love for the British Crown by the people of Trinidad, but judging from conditions, there was not much love for the people of Trinidad by the British Crown.

When Reverend Andrews returned to Fifth Company Village he spoke seriously to the people. He was by far the central figure in Fifth

Company —a much-respected leader by virtue of the fact that he was in charge of the Fifth Company Baptist Church, to which everyone belonged. The forefathers of the villagers were all Baptists, black American ex-soldiers who had been brought to Trinidad by Governor Ralph Woodford in 1816. Woodford had promised the new settlers all manner of development and had promptly forgotten them. They had always been bitter and generations of them had become even more embittered because successive governors and government officials had done nothing for them.

What had hurt most was that Road Board officials for the area spent huge sums of government money every year but not a penny on Fifth Company Village. The roads in the village were narrow tracks—mudholes when the rains came—and all of these tracks had been established by the old settlers and their descendants.

Reverend Andrews, after preaching to the worshippers at the little Baptist church, told them that he was going to appeal to the Road Board no more. Neither would he appeal to the governor, Sir William Robinson. He told them that he was going to send a petition to no less a person than Queen Victoria in London, and he asked their support in signing the petition and getting their friends to sign as well.

The people of Fifth Company Village were enthusiastic as always in following their leader, and Reverend Andrews drafted the petition. He told Queen Victoria of the magnificent displays in San Fernando and throughout Trinidad on the occasion of her Golden Jubilee, and of the touching show of love for her person and for the British Crown. But, he said, there was a painful contrast between their great affection for her and the way the officials she had chosen to represent her carried out their duties.

He recounted a litany of woes suffered by the people of Fifth Company Village—emphasizing the atrocious roads, especially during the rainy season— mentioning how often their children could not go to school because of such conditions, and perhaps the most serious complaint of all: the fact that they could not get produce out of their estates because of the lack of good roads.

Having written the petition, Reverend Andrews got the villagers who knew how to write to sign it, and those who did not know how to write did not have to worry because Reverend Andrews was not slow in signing for them. In fact it seemed as though Reverend Andrews had made friends in San Fernando when he had gone there for the jubilee—and not only friends, but friends of the same turn of mind—for he appeared to have the San Fernando Superintendent of Streets, Julien Maisonneuve, collecting signatures for him through which Maisonneuve lost his job.) When Reverend Andrews had got an impressive number of signatures, he sent the petition to Queen Victoria in London.

Queen Victoria, disturbed by the petition, forthwith directed the Governor of Trinidad, Sir William Robinson, to appoint a Royal Commission to find out what was going on. She particularly asked Sir William Robinson what it was that the people of Fifth Company Village really wanted. In particular, she did not like that part of the petition which asked her to allow the people to choose their own representatives.

Nor did Sir William Robinson and the people he appointed on the Royal Commission. The commissioners were: Stephen Herbert Gatty, the Attorney-General; David Wilson, the Sub-Intendant of Crown Lands; Arthur Wybrow Baker, the Inspector-Commandant of Police; Vincent Brown, Barrister-at-Law; George Lewis Garcia, Barrister-at-Law; Robert Guppy, Mayor of San Fernando; Louis de Verteuil, Member of the Legislative Council; Francis Damian, Mayor of Port-of-Spain; Michel Maxwell Phillips, Solicitor-General; and Henry Brown Phillips, Merchant.

The commissioners, after taking evidence in Port-of-Spain, journeyed to Fifth Company Village to meet the people who had petitioned the Queen and find out what it was that they really wanted.

They interviewed a few of the village-folk whose names were on the list, but it was Reverend Robert Andrews they really wanted to talk to. Many of the people they talked to seemed to be hiding something; there seemed to be something they just were not bringing out. A few of them seemed to have nothing to say, and those who did not really appear to know what a petition was about. A certain number of this last group seemed too illiterate to sign their own names.

But when Reverend Andrews came to the witness stand—a makeshift arrangement inside the little Baptist church—there was no more doubt, no feeling that something was being hidden behind the smiles and the looks of uneasiness and embarrassment. Reverend Andrews answered questions about himself, and he spoke of the background of the village, of how his black American forefathers had come there in 1816, and of how, despite promises, nothing was ever done to improve this settlement. He poured out his complaints about the roads of Fifth Company Village, how when it rained, the children could not go to school, and the produce that could not be brought out of the estates. He complained bitterly of the Road Board officials who left the roads in that awful state.

But the commissioners sensed there was something else behind it all. The chairman, Stephen Herbert Gatty, said to him: "And is that all? If you get good roads, is that all you want?"

Reverend Andrews replied: "By getting good roads, I don't know what may take place hereafter."

And that was it! Reverend Andrews did not know what might take place thereafter. That Commission was a Royal Commission on Franchise—the first—and came about specifically because Reverend Andrews had petitioned Queen Victoria asking her to allow the people to choose their own representatives. The Commissioners, at the end of their enquiry, reported to Sir William Robinson that there was no real desire for the franchise. Sir William, in turn, so informed the Queen. The occasion of 1888 set the question ablaze. The burning desire in the minds of so many turned, in later days, to a widespread flame. It led to the first general election in 1925 (under a partial franchise), then the first adult franchise elections in 1946, and of course, to the big moment of 31 August, 1962, the day that independence came.

CHAPTER THIRTY THREE

THE FIRST TIME WE COULD SAY TRINIDAD AND TOBAGO (1889)

T he first time we were able to use the term "Trinidad and Tobago" was well into the 19th century, when Tobago, in the throes of social unrest and in sudden economic decline, saw itself become linked to Trinidad.

Before this period came along, these two islands followed very different courses. Despite their proximity, they had very different histories. For instance, it is doubtful that Christopher Columbus, who came upon Trinidad in 1498 and claimed it for Spain, even saw Tobago, notwithstanding the fact that he encountered every other island in this area, except Barbados.

Tobago was always the home of the Caribs—a fierce, nomadic tribe of Amerindians, reported to feast on other tribes—while the Amerindian tribes of Trinidad were the peaceful Arawaks. After the first settlement in 1625, Tobago changed hands about a dozen times, but was never Spanish. At various times, it belonged to the British, the French, the Dutch, and once to the Courlanders. Trinidad, before its capture by the British in 1797, was never anything but Spanish. It doesn't seem true, in the light of this, that only twenty two miles of sea separate the two islands.

Tobago first fell to the British in 1762. Shortly before its economic decline, it possessed a political status superior to Trinidad's. It had its own House of Assembly, which meant it could frame its own laws. In other words, it virtually ruled itself.

Trinidad, on the other hand, had been a Crown Colony ever since it came under British colonial rule. Indeed, it was because of islands like Tobago, which, because they were ruled by planters and were opposed to Britain's move to end slavery, that at Trinidad's capture in 1797 Crown Colony government was imposed. This meant that it was run directly from London, rather than by the owners of its plantations.

The two islands continued along their separate courses, both with English-speaking peoples, Trinidad, by virtue of the capture of 1797, as has already been mentioned, and Tobago, because of a final British capture in 1802.

Tobago was reasonably prosperous, until difficulties involving its production of sugar began its economic decline. There was labour unrest, and in 1876, the workers of one of its large estates, Roxborough, rebelled, burning down the house of the estate manager. The manager fled into the bushes while the angry workers went on the rampage. The Roxborough police, under Corporal Belmanna, tried to make arrests, but only succeeded in infuriating the workers further, and now the workers laid siege to the police station. They called for Belmanna, insisting to a high official that he be imprisoned. When, to make peace, the high official relented and was leading Belmanna to the cells, the rioters seized, mutilated and killed him.

Roxborough was in the hands of the rioters for a week, and anarchy spread from there to various parts of Tobago. The authorities, fearing for their lives, somehow managed to get a message out to England, and a short while afterwards, a British warship steamed into Roxborough Bay. To the great surprise of the people, the commander of the warship sent ashore a message of thanks to the people of Roxborough for what he called "keeping the peace", and he invited everyone to come on board to be "decorated". When as many of the villagers as the warship could hold got on board, the warship steamed off to Scarborough, where the people were all put into prison.

The trial of the rioters took many months, and at the end, some of them were given terms of life imprisonment. Others were banished from Tobago.

With the widespread state of crisis, economic decline sharpened. A firm on which the Tobago sugar trade depended heavily—the sugar-planting concern of Gillespie and Company—was now tottering with difficulties, not only because of the labour unrest, but also because of an adjustment in the duties on West Indian and foreign sugar. To add to the problem, there was also a rise in the production of beet sugar in Europe.

The crisis was not only in labour, but in administration too, for just the year before, 1875, the Tobago House of Assembly had abolished itself. The authorities now felt that in the light of the Belmanna unrest, the situation on the island was too volatile to take chances. They had seen that in an emergency they could not keep law and order. So in the dilemma, what did they do? They did the most unusual, but not unexpected, thing: they surrendered their virtual independence, calling on the British authorities to take over responsibility for the island. From the first day of January 1877, Tobago became a Crown Colony, with direct rule from London.

The economic slide continued, and this reached a critical phase—indeed, a point of no return—when Gillespie and Company finally declared itself bankrupt in 1884. They had found that they could not compete with foreign sugar once the preferential treatment for West Indian sugar had been withdrawn, and of course, with beet sugar on the rise in Europe, recovery for the firm was impossible.

When Gillespie and Co. ceased operations, Tobago's economy crashed, and the island became a problem to the British. They could get nothing out of it, and in fact, they now had the responsibility of looking after it. It was a responsibility which they did not want. The Secretary of State for the Colonies now began re-considering a proposal made to him in 1875 by the then administrator of Tobago, Fred Augustus Gore. Administrator Gore, feeling the pinch of the labour crisis and the general frustration which led the House of Assembly to abolish itself, had said on the question of Tobago: "I am of opinion that there is no necessity for maintaining the Colony as a separate Government. The distance from Trinidad to Tobago is only 18 miles, and if a good road were made from Port-of-Spain to Toco and a steam launch employed, daily communication might be established between Port-of-Spain and Scarborough."

This suggestion of 1875 came to mind again, and in 1883, one year before Gillespie and Co. declared itself bankrupt, the British sent a commission to Tobago—the Crossman Commission—to report on the dilemma. The commission's report agreed substantially with the opinion of Fred Augustus Gore that the best move was to unite Trinidad and Tobago administratively. The British government accepted the report, but it was not until January 1887, after a series of official discussions, that an appointed Legislative Council of Tobago approved the measure at a meeting. The Trinidad Legislative Council also met and gave its formal approval.

Events followed fast, and in November 1888, a British Order-in-Council decreed that Trinidad and Tobago be united as one colony as from 1 January, 1889. It was from that date the term "Trinidad and Tobago" could have been used, referring to the two islands as one political unit. Tobago was then under a commissioner. In 1899, Tobago was made a ward of Trinidad.

CHAPTER THIRTYFOUR

THE FIRST TIME ASPHALT (OR PITCH) WAS USED ON OUR STREETS (1890)

W e know that the first publicised use of asphalt, or pitch, dates back to 1595 when Sir Walter Raleigh stopped at the Pitch Lake at La Brea and caulked his leaking ships on his way to El Dorado. Two hundreds years later—in 1795—Governor of Trinidad José Maria Chacón had orders from his superiors to ship asphalt to Spain. The next time we know about asphalt being used was when Governor of Trinidad Ralph Woodford tried it in the 1820s as fuel to light a beacon over Trinity Cathedral.

Of course all this was long before asphalt was dreamed of as a road covering. The first commercial attempt to use asphalt here was in 1850, when Lord Dundonald experimented with asphalt as a fuel for ships. After conducting several experiments in the Gulf of Paria, working out the right ratio of asphalt to coal for efficient performance, he invited Lord Harris on board to watch the experiment. Lord Harris was very impressed with what he saw. However, the venture did not come to anything.

Asphalt did not begin to take on any special significance until 1888, when the American A.L. Barber and other businessmen formed the Trinidad Lake Asphalt Company, primarily for mining and exporting the material. At this time, a suitable covering for roads was being avidly sought, and asphalt was being experimented with. In a short time, asphalt on roads began being commonly used. But not in Trinidad. Although Trinidad possessed the richest source of asphalt in the world, people did not seem to care much about it. In San Fernando, a man called Julien Maisonneuve had an asphalt-refining factory on Broadway for years and pleaded with the San Fernando Borough Council to give asphalt a try. He offered the Borough Council, out of frustration, to pave part of a road for nothing, just to see if they would be pleased and accept asphalt. Julien Maisonneuve , however, made no headway with the San Fernando Borough Council. There were occasions when he went ahead and paved certain parts, hoping for good public reaction, but there was such an outcry that he soon had to desist.

Yet this was the time when a dependable road covering was urgently needed. Macadam, a sort of burnt clay developed by Scotsman John McAdam more than 40 years before, was still the main road covering used. Yet it was far from satisfactory.

As was shown, Trinidad did not take part in the new use of asphalt taking place abroad, but as the 1890s approached, there was the urgent need for a good road covering—a surface that would be more resistant to the wheels of horse-drawn carriages and carts which were beginning to proliferate.

In 1890, the Superintendent of Streets in Port-of-Spain (Town Superintendent) Edward Tanner at last decided to give asphalt a try. The first streets he turned his attention to were Clarence (at the time the upper part of Frederick Street) Frederick Street and Oxford Street. He made them convex, to run off the water, but this proved a particularly sore point. Here is a report from the Port-of-Spain Gazette of 5 April, 1890.

The writer, in discussing the state of the town, says: "Let us take the state of our streets first, where the keynote in successful road-making has been struck in the use of asphalt. The Town Superintendent now cuts an unpopular figure as a carriage-and-horse destroyer with his convex asphalt streets. Clarence Street, Frederick Street and Oxford Street, represent the ... dangerous streets. It is obviously imperative that asphalt streets should be made perfectly flat to put a stop to the mischief they do, and save the Borough Council from a great deal of bitter criticism."

When Tanner left, Walsh Wrightson came as director of Public Works, and he was as bold as Tanner—or even bolder. He fearlessly carried on the good work—or rather, the bad work—for people took a while to be convinced. Horses and mules and other animals of carriage did not feel comfortable with their hooves on the asphalt, but slowly they were becoming accustomed to it. Yet, even while they were becoming accustomed, a new age poised to break was going to welcome this new all-weather surface. Asphalt roads, first experimented with in 1890, soon became widespread because of the advent of motor traffic.

CHAPTER THIRTYFIVE

THE COMING OF ELECTRICITY (1895)

The first move towards introducing electricity as a general service into Trinidad was made in 1892, when Edgar Tripp leased a piece of land from the Borough Council of Port-of-Spain for the purpose of installing an electric plant.

Tripp, a businessman with offices in downtown Port-of-Spain, had the reputation of taking part in all sorts of new business enterprises. The land he leased was part of the old Ariapita Estate, which at one time occupied the entire western side of Port-of-Spain, from St. Vincent Street stretching out to Woodbrook and to the sea. The site of the electric plant was in an area called Shine's Pasture, at that stage well outside the town. Today it is marked by Shine Street. On the eastern side of it, not far from where Stone Street is today, was the Ariapita Asylum or "poor house", and on the other side was the town's dumping ground or La Basse. Tripp had leased this land for $100.00 a year and he lost no time in trying to set up his works.

The Port-of-Spain Borough Council seemed extremely keen about Tripp's proposal to light the town by electricity, for since 1887, they had brought out an Ordinance relating to the manner in which the work was to be carried out. Tripp must have taken this as an affront, for he himself made a number of stipulations, one of which was the removal of the rubbish dump from the area. This rubbish dump was still there in November 1894, as shown by a report of the Borough Council for that month. An extract of the report reads: "Mr. Horsford said he should venture to offer a suggestion in this matter. It seemed to him that the Ariapita Lands were now rather too near the town to continue as a depository ground for the refuse of the city . . . The Borough Council had erected their asylum there, and there was now in the course of erection the large buildings of the Electric Company . . ."

The speaker was David Horsford, Borough Councillor, Member of the Legislative Council, and one of the most influential figures in Port-of-Spain of that day. So perhaps something was going to be done soon.

But Edgar Tripp did not intend to wait on those developments. At that stage, he had already had poles planted in Port-of-Spain and he was busy stringing up wires over the telephone lines. Indeed he had already formed a company, called "The Electric Light and Power Company", registered since 5 July, 1894. He took the job of company secretary, and left the chairmanship to William Gordon Gordon. Other directors included W. S. Robertson, Eugene Cipriani and Lucien F. Ambard.

Not only did Edgar Tripp form a company, but he was already in possession of a contract from the Borough Council. The contract was signed in August 1894, just a month after the company was formed; and strangely enough, the man signing the contract on behalf of the company was not any of the directors, but George Grant. Around this time George Grant went into partnership with William Gordon Gordon, thus forming the firm Gordon, Grant and Company.

But without a doubt, the company in the public eye was the Electric Light and Power Company, and its contract of August 1894 stipulated that Port-of-Spain was to be lit by electricity as from 5 March, 1895. Towards the end of 1894, Edgar Tripp was still having wires strung up on his tall pitchpine poles. The officials of the Telephone Company, a concern which itself had not too long been established, took great exception to the work of the new electric concern. The electric company was using its own poles, nevertheless the telephone people were very much in opposition, objecting to the electric wires being strung above theirs. The reason they gave was that if the two sets of lines came into contact this could cause a fire at the telephone exchange. Other people shared that anxiety, for a few months previously, Councillor Mzumbo Lazare had declared at a Borough Council meeting: "Would any agreement for the electric lighting of the town stipulate that the wires be run underground instead of overhead?"

But Lazare had been told that it was too late to make that stipulation.

At that stage the equipment for the electric engines was being installed by Mr. Kuhn, the engineer, who was putting in four engines to run dynamos. The boiler was also going up. So far as the wire-men were concerned, Tripp was having the Borough Council lop off the tops of the trees in Marine Square so as not to be in the way of the wires.

Thus the new year, 1895, opened with the prospect of brighter things. Certainly brighter than the oil lamps which lit Port-of-Spain. There was gas, too, but only a few places had that. The gasworks were at La Fantasie, St. Ann's, and as could be expected, the Governor's Residence (now the President's House) was among the few places that benefited.

The entire town was now going to benefit from electric light, Tripp had said. People had completely rejected oil, as can be seen from the following newspaper comment of around that time: "That the capital of La Belle Trinidad ... should, up to this moment in the matter of street lighting, use an illuminant of the commonest and most primitive type, to wit, oil, seems to us incongruous and astonishing."

But although everyone looked forward to what Edgar Tripp's effort would bring, his opponents were as determined as ever to stop him. For instance, on 22 February, 1895, Chairman of the Commercial Telephone Company, Conrad F. Stollmeyer, asked in the Legislative Council: "Is Government satisfied that all reasonable precautions have been taken against the risk of accident to life in the erection of the overhead wires in the streets of Port-of-Spain?"

Walsh Wrightson, who had just arrived as Director of Public Works, and who was still far from constructing his Wrightson Road, put everyone at ease by saying the overhead wires were no problem at all. He had seen that all over the world, he said.

That took place on 22 February, 1895, and on the following Tuesday the great moment came. Edgar Tripp's contract stipulated that lights should be turned on no later than midnight on Tuesday, 5 March, 1895, but Tripp's work was so advanced that on Tuesday, 26 February—one week before—he was able to give a demonstration to eager crowds. People were stunned when the lights were switched on, and a news report said: "There was a great deal of enthusiasm shown by the crowds on the streets when the lights first shone forth and great crowds collected under each lamp and discussed the characteristics of this new agency by which night is to be made more like day."

The first English cricket team to come to Trinidad—Slade Lucas and his Englishmen—were in Port-of-Spain, and the governor's wife, Lady Napier Broome, had asked for the demonstration so that they could have a night drive through the streets.

Edgar Tripp went around town, inspecting the work, but it was more like a lap-of-honour than an inspection, for crowds cheered him and shook his hand wherever he went. Especially was this so at the Medical Hall, near the junction of Park and St. Vincent Streets (today's Green Corner) where large crowds all but took him away, and gave him a burst of applause for a job well done.

EDGAR TRIPP & CO.,
Trinidad, B.W.I.

LEFT: ELECTRICITY PIONEER EDGAR TRIPP

BELOW: FREDERICK STREET LOOKING SOUTH WITH TRAM LINES AND WIRING FOR TELEPHONE AND ELECTRICITY.

The next Tuesday, 5 March, 1895, Port-of-Spain was officially lit up by electricity. Some of the first buildings to have electric lights by this time was the Governor's Residence (President's House), the Queen's Park Hotel, only finished that January, and the Princes Building.

CHAPTER THIRTY SIX

THE FIRST ELECTRIC TRAMS (1895)

A
fter electricity first lit certain streets of Port-of-Spain on 5 March, 1895, it was only a matter of time before the Electric Company made its presence felt not only with electric light but with power. Soon after that grand occasion, the company formed a subsidiary called "The Electric Light, Power, and Tramway Company."

This name of course let everyone know what the company's intention was. It was going to turn its attention to running trams. Up to then, trams were run by mules, and it was not far in the past when great crowds had gathered in front of the railway station on South Quay to watch the start of the mule tram service. It will be recalled that a reporter had described the mules as moving "in excellent style".

But events moved faster, and the excellent style of 1883 lost its lustre before the developments of 1895, especially so far as electricity was concerned. Everybody knew, from the newspapers, that the tramway company had imported electric trams, and so the mule tram service, inaugurated only in 1883, was already regarded as old-fashioned and out-of-date.

People waited excitedly as they saw an electric tram depot go up on the eastern side of the Queen's Park Savannah, and following its completion, they did not have to wait long before action came. The date was 26 June, 1895, when Lady Broome—wife of then Governor Sir Frederick Napier Broome—went from Government House to "the junction of the St. Ann's and Belmont Roads" to start the first electric tram service.

Cheering crowds lined the route from the Upper Belmont Circular Road junction towards town, all along Charlotte Street. Apart from the rank and file, almost all the dignitaries of Port-of-Spain were there to witness Lady Broome perform the ceremony. At four in the afternoon the three trams were drawn up at the terminus. To match the holiday atmosphere, the trams were all decorated with flags, buntings and bouquets of flowers. In front of the cheering crowds, Lady Broome gave the signal and the trams started off on their first run. A reporter on the spot wrote: "The rate of speed was fairly high, fully 15 miles an hour—but there was no motion of any unpleasant character, and all were delighted with the ease at which the (tram) cars sped along."

And this was travelling in really excellent style! People so fell in love with this form of transport that by 1902 the company was seeking to establish eight new lines in Port-of-Spain. A line around the Queen's Park Savannah—called the belt line—was started that year.

After the 20th century opened, the electric tram ran its course through four decades before finally coming to the end of the line. Following the takeover of the Electric Company in 1937, the Trinidad Electricity Board and the Port-of-Spain City Council were engaged in a bitter dispute over the concern, and this speedily brought an end to the trams. The Trinidad Electricity Board, which was to hand over part of the Electric Company to the Corporation, declined to repair the tram lines for years, and the service became dangerous. City Councillor L.B. Thomas said in 1945: "I have never seen the tracks in such a bad condition, and I have seen the first tram run in Port-of-Spain."

That very year, 1945, the Trinidad Electricity Board was to hand over the Port-of-Spain part of the concern to the Port-of-Spain Corporation, and now this authority, called the Corporation Electricity

A Tramcar crossing Henry Street looking South.

Board, became the authority for running the trams. But it could not run the trams without trained staff, and the Trinidad Electricity Board refused to hand over the staff which had run the trams.

The last trams rolled away at the very end of 1945, which meant the service had lasted 50 years. No doubt L.B. Thomas watched them sadly and recalled that day of 26 June, 1895, when hundreds of excited people cheered the first electric trams to run in Trinidad.

CHAPTER THIRTY SEVEN

THE FIRST MOTOR CAR ON OUR STREETS (1900)

T he paving of Port-of-Spain's streets with asphalt in the 1890s prepared the town for a very special event, an event which came in 1900.

It happened in March, a most eventful month in Port-of-Spain's history. For example, Port-of-Spain had burned down twice in the month of March—in 1808 and again in 1895. Electricity came in March 1895, the Red House was burned down in March 1903, St. Joseph Convent was inaugurated in March 1836, and Queen's Royal College was opened in March 1904, to name a few events. Now once again in March something happened which jolted the attention. The date is 24 March, 1900, and the newspapers of the following day broke the news: "Yesterday, for the first time, an automobile was witnessed here traversing the streets, with Messrs Garner and Khun as occupants. It was observed by everybody with unmixed pleasure. We are pretty certain it will not be long before these horseless carriages will be in great use locally."

The term "horseless carriages" was a most appropriate term, for it was the first time in the history of Trinidad that a carriage was seen traversing the streets without being drawn by a horse.

This event was of course the appearance of the first car in Trinidad. Crowds gathered to see Mr. Garner and Mr. Khun drive by, but although everybody viewed this horseless carriage with unmixed pleasure, few believed it was anything more than an unexplained stunt. Even the reporter that day was not alive to a sense of history, for he neither mentions where he saw the carriage, nor who are Messrs. Garner and Khun. A few days later, however, when the horseless carriage proved to be the talk of the town, he went to inspect the machine and to talk to the owner, Mr. Garner.

In an article entitled: "A Look around the Locomobile," the author goes into a detailed description of how works this first motor car to appear in Trinidad, and in a part of the article he says: "The body, which completely encloses the machinery, is suspended on a frame of 10" gauge tubing by means of a transverse laminated plate spring at the front, and two springs of the same type at the back. Above the two axles the springs are securely bolted."

If to some engineers today the simplified description fits a box cart, it was much more than that, for in speaking of the radiator he says: "The boiler consists of a number of solid drawn copper tubes, and is placed under the seat of the carriage."

Maybe the reader that day would have been puzzled to hear that the carriage worked by gasoline—for he would hardly have known what that was, the liquid not yet being produced in the Trinidad of that time. The machine took three gallons of the fuel. To find the "storage tank" one would have had to look beneath the footboard.

The general reader might have wanted to know, first of all, how much Mr. Garner had paid for the carriage, and where it came from. Information advanced, like: "There is a hand brake which stops this car", might not have meant much, nor might it have helped him to be told: "The engine is located in front of the boiler and is secured to the frame of the body. The frame is of brass, and a special feature is that the engine has ball bearings."

The reader would have been interested to know that Mr. Garner had paid 960 dollars for the automobile, and that it was imported from Boston. The car had two seats. The wheels were rather big—three feet in diameter, and there was only a half-inch wad of tyre around them. The viewer, although he could see no horse, would have been

ONE OF THE FIRST PROUD OWNERS
OF A MOTORCAR IN TRINIDAD.

reminded of the animal by the words printed on the engine: Three horse-power. So the engine had the power of three horses! No wonder that the reporter, after describing the process of starting the car, declared: "The carriage can now leave the stable."

Messrs Garner and Khun stole the limelight so far as transport was concerned, but not for very long. And this fact was anticipated by a statement in the Port-of-Spain Gazette. It said: "Probably the day is not far off when these carriages will be common in the Island of Trinidad. Already one of our leading dry goods merchants has ordered one."

CHAPTER ThirtyEight

THE FIRST APPEARANCE OF CARNIVAL BANDS(1900)

A lthough Carnival, as an all-pervading festival of the masses, began as early as 1839—after slavery was abolished and the masses could come out onto the streets—the festival did not change much with the succeeding years, but remained a display of tumultuous revelry, and there was little of the pageantry and spectale of our own day. Before 1839, Carnival had been very limited in participation, of course, for the French who introduced it never celebrated on the streets, but instead with exquisite disguise balls in their own great houses.

There were about 10,000 free blacks at this point in time, and it is true that some of them did come out onto the streets to celebrate Carnival, but this was never approved of by the authorities. Bearing in mind that in those days the festivities started from the Saturday night, here is a report from the Port-of-Spain Gazette of 22 January, 1833: "On Sunday afternoon an attempt was made by Mr. Peake to check the shameful violation of the Sabbath by the lower order of the population, who are accustomed at this time of year to wear masks and create disturbances on a Sunday."

But the fact was that even if it were Carnival Monday, Mr. Peake, who was assistant to the Police Chief, would have stopped the lower classes under the pretext of preserving order. However, after 1839 it would not have been so easy. Yet there is no denying that the story of Carnival from 1839 to the late years of the 19th century is a story of wild revelry and license, and despite some innocent scenes of joy and merriment on the streets, it was really the best time in Trinidad for anyone contemplating mischief or violence. And with the wearing of masks, one could, in the true meaning of the term, get away with murder.

Also, because of the tension and bitterness between the classes—a legacy of slavery - it was a favourite time for the masses to declare war on the authorities, especially the police. And the police seemed to look forward to Carnival to obtain good exercise in baton-swinging! The history of Carnival is full of bloody confrontations.

The most celebrated of these clashes happens to be the one that changed Carnival for good. This was the occasion of the Cannes Brulées (Canboulay) riots of 1881. "Cannes Brulées", a term that means "burning cane", was a flambeau procession to commemorate the burning of canefields in the time of slavery. At such times, slave-masters got slaves from all the surrounding estates to put out the fire. The commemoration of "Cannes Brulées" was innocent enough, but the authorities regarded it as highly dangerous because of the risk of fire. Yet this was the most popular of all Carnival activities and the revellers, sensitive to the fact that the police were always ready to harrass them, had no intention of stopping.

At Carnival in 1881 the police, under Captain Baker, forbade Canboulay revellers to come out, but in the early hours of Carnival Monday morning the revellers appeared, in defiance of the police. Captain Baker and his men attacked them with great force and brutality and there was widespread and bloody rioting in Port-of-Spain. The Canboulay revellers were routed.

That morning, a delegation of masqueraders went to complain to Governor Sir Sanford Freeling, who listened to them sympathetically. In the afternoon, he came down to the marketplace on George Street to address the masqueraders. On that occasion, addressing them as "My friends", he told them that it was not the intention to stop their enjoyment. He said, "It was the fear of fire that caused the police to stop you." He told them that he would confine the police to barracks and they could masquerade to their heart's content, once they did not burn down the town.

Of course, Freeling incurred the wrath of the Colonial Office in London for having done this, and was recalled, but his action had an overwhelming effect on the Carnival and the festival was never to be the same again. The masquerading masses—the so-called lower orders—were amazed that the governor could have come out so openly on their side, and in a way this transformed them. At the next Carnival, the following notice was posted about the town by Carnival groups: "Advice for Carnival 1882. Let us not let down Governor Freeling, who gave us the freedom to play the Carnival. Remember the pains His Excellency took to come down to your market square last year?" It called on masqueraders to abstain from any kind of violence as a mark of appreciation to Governor Freeling.

Shortly after Carnival 1882, the Port-of-Spain Gazette, always hostile to Carnival, had the following report: "The Carnival of 1882 has come and gone and the results have proved what every man, woman, and child, outside the police authorities, know, but what Captain Baker does not know, or affects not to know, namely, that there is not in any country a population more naturally peaceable ... and amenable to reason and good advice than the people of Trinidad."

The fact was that from this time onwards the tone of Carnival had changed. At Carnival no longer was the accent placed on tumult and violence. Instead, people began concentrating on having a good time and looking good. Now that they were not going out onto the streets to fight, they could dress up, for their nice clothes would not be ruined. The silks and satins began to emerge.

This change became marked in the 1890s and significantly enough, the 1890s saw the advent of asphalt roads. It is safe to assume that the disappearance of dusty, muddy roads brought out the flowing and colourful costumes even more profusely. Since bright and colourful costumes looked better when they appeared in numbers and were uniform, it led to a further development: people dressing the

MELTON PRIOR'S FAMOUS DRAWING OF CARNIVAL IN PORT-OF-SPAIN

same way set out to depict a certain idea. This struck the attention at Carnival 1900, and a news report appearing on 28 February that year (just after the Carnival) said: "A marked feature of this year's Carnival has been the general adoption of the idea of combination into bands, each with a distinctive banner, bearing a title and motto."

This was the birth of Carnival bands as we know them today. Although the trend was seen as early as the 1890s, we can safely point to the Carnival of 1900 as the first time costumed Carnival bands came out on the streets.

THIRTYNINE
CHAPTER

THE FIRST TIME OIL WAS FOUND IN COMMERCIAL QUANTITIES (1902)

I t was in the year 1902 that the determined oil prospector, Randolph Rust, after years of hard work in the Guayaguayare forests, and weary of drilling "dry holes", at last struck oil and brought it to the surface.

In those days, Guayaguayare, lying as it does in the south-eastern corner of Trinidad, was easily one of the remotest areas of the island. Randolph Rust had gone there prospecting for oil some years after a surveyor had reported oil seepages in the forest. The surveyor, George Reginald Gilkes, had taken a sample of the liquid to a friend, a shop-keeper called John Lee Lum. Lee Lum took it to Randolph Rust, then a merchant in Port-of-Spain. The sample was sent to analysts in London and the glowing report on this high-grade sample of petroleum sparked off great enthusiasm on the part of Randolph Rust. He was determined to drill for oil in the Guayaguayare forests.

It was a formidable task that Rust had undertaken.

Guayaguayare was particularly inaccessible. There were no roads leading to the district, except a track from Mayaro, which in many instances depended on the beach, and therefore on the tides. It hardly needs to be said that all the heavy equipment to be brought in to Guayaguayare had to be brought in by sea, and with no proper harbour this was a precarious exercise.

Rust made the best of very adverse circumstances, so far as bringing in the equipment was concerned, and he and his helpers roamed the thick, vermin-infested forests, drilling holes wherever oil seemed likely. And presto! One lucky day in July 1902, oil spewed to the surface in the wake of his drill. Rust seemed crazed with joy. As soon as he could get out of Guayaguayare, he hurried to Port-of-Spain to break the news.

Rust's success created a great stir in government and industrial circles in Port-of-Spain. The mechanical age had just set in; automobiles were being invented and these and other machines were using oil and products of oil as fuel, and so oil was getting to be in great demand in the world. The Trinidad authorities felt that if Trinidad was to prove to possess this valuable resource, then what lay ahead was a bright and most exciting day. Trinidad was going to move from being one of a number of poor West Indian islands to occupy a special place in this part of the world.

With the sudden flaring up of interest, Rust invited a few people to see for themselves. Governor Sir Alfred Maloney was not in Trinidad at this time, but Rust's party was headed by the Acting Governor, Sir Courtenay Knollys. It included the Governor's Private Secretary, Drury Wake; Acting Director of Public Works, Percival Stevens; Rust's wife, and some members of the press. The party left by steamer from Port-of-Spain, taking the southerly route to Guayaguayare.

The journey proved to be an exceptionally long one in the context of today, but perhaps not too much so in the context of 1902. The steamer, having left Port-of-Spain at 1 p.m. in the afternoon, and in favourable weather, did not arrive at La Brea until 4.30 p.m. After a delay at La Brea of two hours waiting for the engineer of the works, Mr. Mosher, they left La Brea at 7 p.m., and seemed to have rounded Icacos Point around midnight. Daylight found them not yet past Moruga, and they did not arrive in Guayaguayare Bay until 9.30 a.m. on Sunday morning. They anchored half a mile from the shore, just opposite the mouth of the Mot River. The waters of the bay were choppy and full of swells, but despite the long journey, this only seemed to add to the excitement of being at Guayaguayare and being near to the oil find. The boats bringing the party ashore rushed through the spray and haze of the breakers, and then the visitors found themselves riding high on brawny backs which brought them on to dry sand. By about 10.30 a.m. everybody was safely ashore.

There was a welcoming party on Guayaguayare beach with flags and flowers, and with schoolchildren singing patriotic songs, and now there was the booming of guns to greet the Acting Governor.

From there, corials (canoe-like boats) took the party up-river, a distance of about two and a half miles. After being paddled through dark and damp high woods they came to a carat-roofed "ajoupa" which was the camp of the oil pioneers, near to the oil well. After a brief rest and repast, the party proceeded to examine the well.

"At first sight," wrote one of the reporters, "the well is perhaps a little disappointing, the mouth consisting of a circular piece of iron tubing, about four to six inches in diameter, sunk in the ground. Around and above it however, is an immense iron-frame scaffolding 72 feet in height, from the wheeldrum at the top of which hangs by a steel-wire a four-inch auger stamp with which the well was bored. This being removed, there is substituted for it a peculiar dipper in the shape of a long steel tube, stopped at the lower end with a valve, which, on being let down into the well, fills with oil, and then returning full of oil is diverted into a barrel nearby."

The reporter continued: "Here the valve, striking the bottom of the cask, is forced up, and the 20 gallons of black, oily stuff, rushes out, half filling the barrel, and passing by a tube thence into the storage tanks some distance off, while the dipper is hauled back,the valve re-closes, and the whole swings back into the well for the next supply. The well was drilled to a depth of about 850 feet."

So deep in the Guayaguayare forests Randolph Rust had a quite complicated set up. The reporter also mentioned petroleum gas rushing out of the well as soon as the pumping begins, and he informed that the striking of a match could be disastrous. After leaving Rust's derrick, the group visited his surface lake of petroleum, which was the reservoir, 10 feet deep, filled with oil which the reporter, more familiar with sugar estates, likened to molasses.

He continued: "The next move was to visit some curious holes in the ground, where, through bubbling springs of oily water the petroleum gas is escaping constantly, in such quantities as to be easily lit with a match. The bubbling of the gas as it escapes from below, through the water, causes a boiling sound audible for several yards, showing considerable pressure to exist from below, and Mr. Rust stated one such hole where he lit the gas burned for weeks."

This is the natural gas so much in demand today. In those days, those "curious holes" were well-known in Guayaguayare, especially by the huntsmen, who were said to cook their meals over them. The reporter learned this too, no doubt from Randolph Rust, for he wrote: "The existence of these gas holes . . . has been known to the residents and hunters for years, one man stating he had often heard of woodmen utilising these natural gas stoves for cooking . . . But apparently little or no attention has been hitherto paid to them."

The party, after drinking several toasts to the new oil industry, and expressing the hope that it would transform the economy of the country, got into the corials again, and sailed down-river to the beach. It was about 3 o'clock in the afternoon when they left the oil wells. They got back to the steamer, and left Guayaguayare Bay around 6 p.m. They arrived in Port-of-Spain at 7.30 a.m. on Monday morning.

The Port-of-Spain Gazette said of the oil discovery: "The finding of petroleum oil in Mayaro is certain to be one of the most fortunate things to have befallen this Colony . . . It is impossible to imagine what a change for the better may not in the next few years come over the hitherto almost primitive districts of Mayaro and Guayaguayare."

CHAPTER FORTY

THE FIRST BUSES (1910)

U p to the end of the 19th century, the transporting of passengers in Trinidad was by means of animal traffic, the railway train, or, since 1895 in Port-of-Spain, the electric tram. Ever since the first motor car made its appearance in 1900, the idea of transporting passengers by motor vehicles must have been in the mind, but it was not before 1910 that the first motor omnibus, or motor bus, as it was called, appeared on the streets.

One of the first motor bus services in Trinidad was run by the Siparia businessman Asgaralli Syne, and it was a service that plied between Siparia and San Fernando, although it often appeared to run to St. James in Port-of-Spain, where Syne had quarters, and sometimes as far South as Icacos, where he also had quarters.

Syne's bus service, and one a little before, Newallo's, appear to have been entirely alone right up to the beginning of the First World War, and of course during the war the importation of vehicles was seriously curtailed, but it was when that war ended that the picture suddenly changed. Between 1900 and 1914, there must have been only about one hundred motor vehicles in Trinidad, yet by January 1920 there were 1,176 vehicles registered.

It was at that time, because of the rapid increase in the number of motor vehicles, that the authorities began to frame legislation for the licensing, use and control of these vehicles. Up to 1919, a great number of vehicles travelled without headlights, on account of the headlights being defective, and so regulations about having headlights tested came out in 1919.

As could be imagined, at this stage Syne's Bus Service was no longer alone, and in January 1920, one was confronted with the following notice: "Prior to any motor lorry or motor bus being used on any public road, the owner of such lorry or bus shall first obtain a permit in writing from the District Engineer of the Public Works Department who has charge of the particular road over which it is intended that traffic shall take place."

But although there were buses around, bus services were still very few, so much so that a reporter wrote the following with relish in early 1920: "We are informed that a motor bus service between Four Roads and Macqueripe is soon to be inaugurated by Mr. Charles Ross of Ross' Bazaars. Such a service is sure to be hailed with delight—especially by those persons who have no other vehicle than the tram car."

Mr. Ross' new service seemed to have been a signal for a number of other bus services, and this could be guessed at by the amount of motor vehicles which came into the country between January 1520 and November 1921.

Although only 1,176 vehicles had been registered by mid-January 1920, there were already 2,000 vehicles registered by November 1921. Of these 824 new vehicles, motor trucks and motor buses must have been well represented. Buses at this time were becoming a serious challenge to the railway, and to underline this, on 16 February, 1923, Governor S.H. Wilson told the Legislative Council: "I regret to say that in the year which has just closed there has been a further large decrease in the number of passengers carried by the railway. This decrease can be attributed partly to trade depression and partly to competition from motor vehicles."

The competition to the railway train was mainly from the motor bus, for few members of the travelling public had cars in 1923. By the mid-1920s, the bus was the great vehicle of public transport all over Trinidad. In Port-of-Spain, wherever there was a bus-stand, tumult reigned. At one bus-stand in Marine Square dispute and fist fights among different bus crews were the order of the day, due to their constant wrangle to get passengers. Travellers around these places often found themselves pushed into buses under protest. Very often the buses sped away with passengers who desired to go by other buses. (The expression "sped away" must be taken in the context of the 1920s. The magistrate's court was daily filled with drivers charged with "driving in excess of 25 miles per hour", the speed limit of the time.)

So the bus as the main vehicle of transport for passengers came into its own in the 1920s. It had not been a very long road to travel, considering that it was only just past the first decade of the century, when Newallo, and then Asgaralli Syne—both of Siparia—had led the way with the first bus services in Trinidad.

CHAPTER FORTYONE

THE FIRST CINEMA (1911)

THE FIRST CINEMA (1911)

The earliest cinema in Trinidad opened its doors in French Street, Woodbrook, on Thursday, 2 February, 1911. It was a wonderful and emotional evening, and people came from all parts of the country to see what the advertisements had described as "The World Before Your Eyes".

They had arrived from distant villages by train and by horse-and-cart, and those on the outskirts had come by trams and cabs and some on foot. Everyone was eager to witness this amazing new advance in science whereby pictures of events in the outside world could be flashed on the screen before one's very eyes.

It was a wonderful evening because of the event, but certainly not so far as the weather was concerned, because it was a very rainy day. Yet the crowds converged on French Street, and the building they headed for was the London Electric Theatre, which was on the corner of French Street and Baden-Powell Street, just on the edge of the Woodbrook Savannah. The building, now a church, is still there today. The London Electric Theatre, or cinema-theatre as it really was, opened its doors to these great crowds at 8 p.m., and the programme comprised nine picture sequences, including titles such as "The Leopard Queen", "Kidnapped Mother-in-Law", as well as current news and events.

Of course the images were merely stills, for there was no such thing as movement on the screen—the motion picture or "movie" being as yet undreamed of. At this stage few thought such a thing possible. Nor was there any such thing as sound coming from the screen itself, for this was the remotest period of the silent days of the cinema-screen. The music the crowd heard was from a piano placed beside the screen and the man at the keyboard was Lanky Belasco, famous musician and entertainer, who was to become a legend in this field during those "silent" days. Lanky accompanied the picture stories with glad or sad music as the occasion demanded. That day, Thursday, 2 February, 1911, was a great occasion for him, not only because of his playing, but because the cinema was partly owned by him.

On that first day there were many scores of specially invited guests, but those paying would have had to find 24 cents, 16 cents, or eight cents, depending on where they had chosen to sit. They could go to balcony, stalls, or pit. Whatever they paid, though, or wherever they sat, they would certainly have felt that they got their money's worth. There were showers of applause. Next morning, the Port-of-Spain Gazette called the performance both entertaining and instructive. It was a most extraordinary experience, and none guessed then that the babes-in-arms who must have been there that evening would see much greater miracles in the years not far ahead of them.

The popularity of the London Electric Theatre was so great that it could hardly accommodate the crowds – especially when the First World War came three years later and right there on the screen people could see the action that had taken place on the battle front. It was not surprising that under these circumstances Lanky Balasco, a king pin of the London Electric Theatre, should find grounds in 1916 for quarrelling with his colleagues and breaking away. Knowing the business as he did, he opened the second cinema in Port-of-Spain. Together with a Miss Doris Legge, he opened in Belmont, at the corner of Erthig Road and Pelham Street, a cinema called the Olympic Theatre.

That very year, 1916, attracted yet another figure who was to try his fortune in the cinema business. He was the American George

Rosenthal, who leased St. Ann's Hall on Oxford Street to give Port of-Spain the "City Cinema". Since Port-of-Spain had become a city only two years before—in 1914—the name must have sounded especially apt at the time.

But the London Electric Cinema was not dead! It continued to provide a stage for the unusual and for the great. All the gifted artists who were passing through Trinidad, as well as local stars who were rising, all the top performers—pianists, conjurers, clowns, singers, dancers, actors and actresses, jugglers, magic men; all these people who thrilled the Port-of-Spain of the time would be sure to have thrilled it from the stage of the London Electric Theatre. Of course, gone were the days when great crowds would come from the most distant villages as well as from various parts of Port-of-Spain to rush to its gas-lit halls, for it was no longer the only such place of entertainment in the town, and it no longer had the monopoly of the celluloid reels. It remained a magic name for years. However, as the 1920s came in, the London Electric Theatre showed signs of wilting—especially in the face of the competition provided by George Rosenthal.

Yet Rosenthal himself could not take the competition he had to withstand, and film-lovers saw him hit back by putting up what was the first tarpaulin cinema in Trinidad. This was at the northeastern corner of Edward Street and Tragarete Road in Port-of-Spain. He called it the "Empire Theatre". This makeshift theatre did so well that Rosenthal was able to construct a solid Empire Theatre soon afterwards. He opened the new building on 25 September, 1930.

This shifted the scene and now it was to this stage the great performers came. One of its big successes of the period was the great singer Alyce Fraser, who drew crowds to the Empire Theatre to hear her perform.

After 1920 the scene changed swiftly. First William Humphrey joined Rosenthal to form the Colonial Film Exchange. In the end Humphrey bought over Rosenthal's share and became the powerful figure of Trinidad cinema-theatres.

Humphrey was challenged by the American Film Company, Metro-Goldwyn-Mayer, who backed a newcomer, Gokool Meah, helping

ONE OF THE FIRST CINEMAS, THE ROYAL THEATRE, COR. OBSERVATORY AND CHARLOTTE STREETS.

him to build a cinema in Port-of-Spain. Of course the understanding was that this cinema would show only Metro-Goldwyn-Mayer's films. Gokool naturally called the cinema "Metro", but soon becoming irate over the restriction, and wanting to show whatever film he pleased, he broke with Metro-Goldwyn-Mayer and called his cinema "Globe". The cinema, with the original name, Metro, was opened on 19 March, 1933.

And 1933 was time for the new man on the scene, Timothy Roodal, to step in and build his "Roxy Theatre". Roxy was opened on 13 October, 1934. By now not only the movies but the talkies were here. In fact the first "talking" (and moving) film was shown by Tucker Trinitone Movies on 15 January, 1930. The film was called "Flight".

Yet it is neither sound nor silence in films that we recall now. The moment we recall is 8 p.m. on Thursday, 2 February, 1911, when, with the opening of the London Electric Theatre, Trinidad got a cinema for the first time.

CHAPTER FORTYTWO

THE FIRST ATTEMPT AT AIR FLIGHT IN TRINIDAD (1913)

T he first attempt in Trinidad to fly through the air in a machine was made just after the first decade of this century began.

The man making this attempt was an American called Frank Boland. In 1913, flying in a machine through the air was one of the great and remarkable novelties, and as yet few were the men who were brave enough to attempt it. Frank Boland arrived here with a bright hot fame, for in a bi-plane of his own invention he had toured South America and had drawn thunderous cheers for having actually gone up into the air.

When the air hero arrived here, crowds of people went to the Queen's Park Savannah to see him and his airplane, for the this was the venue from which he would show his skill.

The machine which, with Boland, had caused such a sensation, was tail-less and no more than six feet long. It was placed inside of a tent and was to stay there until the day of the demonstration, and the crowds of people who turned up to see it had to pay one shilling to go into the tent. However, everybody saw it to advantage a few days later, for that day, Thursday, 23 January, 1913, was to be the day of the great demonstration.

Port-of-Spain was gripped with excitement. People had seen many wonders of late years but nothing could be more wonderful than what they were expecting to see that morning. In March 1900 they had seen the first "horseless carriage"—the motor car. But as strange as that experience was, no vehicle moving on the ground could be as spectacular as one moving through air!

As the crowd massed, the bi-plane was brought out of the tent and placed to the east of the ground, somewhere near to where the grandstand is now.

It was nearing 9 o'clock, the hour for the demonstration. Boland, dressed in dungarees and wearing air-bells, stood near to the little one-seater machine, while the crowd held its breath in anticipation.

Governor George Le Hunte was specially invited to witness the feat, but he, too, seemed nervous, and he was whiling away the time playing tennis on the grounds of Government House. As it approached 9 o'clock, he walked across the grounds and came towards Frank Boland. Sir George shook hands with Frank Boland, wishing him luck, and then, amidst cheers, the aviator went into the cockpit of the tiny machine. He started the engine, and now there was a hush in the crowd. The propeller went whirling round and then the little air-plane sped westward along the green.

The machine then stopped, and the aviator directed Governor George Le Hunte to a point of vantage. The bi-plane now darted eastward, and amidst deafening cheers, it lifted off. A reporter of the Port-of-Spain Gazette described the flight of those few seconds: "A truly magnificent spectacle is presented as the skillful aviator soars aloft, steering his way amongst the trees that lay in his route."

The aviator saluted some friends on the ground as the little plane sped towards the north-western end of the savannah, barely above the tree-tops. The crowd watched spellbound. Then, just before the bi-plane reached the north-western rim of the Queen's Park Savannah, it suddenly dipped, then crashed to the ground.

This was by far the most dramatic tragedy in Trinidad for the year 1913. The plane crashed near what is called "The Hollows" in the Queen's Park Savannah. One of the medical men in Port-of-Spain, a

Dr. Lota, saw the crash from a passing tram-car and rushed to the scene, later to be followed by a Dr. Suing. The plane had crashed from about 70 feet—the highest it had got to—but this was enough to mangle and pitch the body of the aviator, Frank Boland, about 35 feet away from the wreckage. No need to say that the airman was killed instantaneously.

Boland's body was placed in Dr. Suing's car and taken to the Colonial Hospital, with throngs of people in its wake. There, after the formalities of certifying his death, and other such matters, Father Sutherland performed the last rites. The funeral took place on Friday, 24 January, 1913, the day after the crash.

The body of the 36-year-old Frank Boland left the Colonial Hospital for Rosary Church, and afterwards it was taken to Lapeyrouse Cemetery for burial.

This closed the chapter on the tragedy attending man's first attempt at aviation in Trinidad.

CHAPTER FORTY THREE

THE FIRST INDUSTRIAL STRIKE (1919)

T he first industrial strike in Trinidad occurred at the end of the First World War, when the return of the soldiers from the front, severe economic depression and rampant unemployment changed the entire picture of industrial affairs in this country.

Following the joyful, emotional months of peace, which came on the heels of the armistice of November 1918, gloom set in, and with the return of the ex-soldiers the entire year 1919 was one of unrest. For the soldiers, who had risked their lives fighting for "king and country", did not accept kindly that the prize for risking their lives seemed to be unemployment and squalor. However, their rebelliousness drew the censure of the authorities.

Entering the fray on the men's behalf was a very resolute and determined leader, a veritable captain of the people. This was Arthur Andrew Cipriani, who had led these men in the West India Regiment during the war. He had inspired the men overseas and had seen them fight in the most heroic way, and his dream had been to see them return to a land fit for heroes to live in. Who had ever heard of such ideas? These men, for whom there had been a triumphal arch on the jetty on their return, and for whom the band had played "Home Sweet Home", and who had heard Governor John Chancellor praise them for having offered to "sacrifice their lives"—these men were quickly forgotten by the authorities and had to take their places in the bread line. Indeed, the first of them had arrived on 26 May, 1919, and as early as 21 July, 1919, at a huge Peace Day rally on the Queen's Park Savannah, the bitterness of the ex-soldiers had broken out in violence. The Trinidad Guardian of Wednesday, 23 July, reported: "The occasion of the peace celebration in Port-of-Spain on Monday was marred by a series of disgraceful incidents in which a number of returned soldiers, aided by a crowd of roughs, got completely out of hand . . ."

The report told of pandemonium as far away as Prince Street, and went on: "Bottles and other missiles and sticks and razors were the weapons of offence, and many people who live in the vicinity of the fight had to close their windows and doors in order to be secure from the rain of stones."

This continued to be the pattern wherever the ex-soldiers were involved. Cipriani knew that this was not the answer. He called on the ex-soldiers and they rallied to him. He saw the attitude of the employers and of the government as crass and callous, and he said so without fear. He saw a trial of strength developing between Labour and Capital and he took up the challenge. He at once closed ranks, not only with the men he had led in the war, but with the working class in general.

In that year, 1919, Cipriani felt that so far as workers' grievances were concerned, everything depended on the solidarity of the workers themselves. With unemployment being rampant, the workers had to accept the worst possible conditions in order to keep their jobs. Cipriani would have none of this. He revived the old Trinidad Workingmen's Association—an association which had been founded in 1897 by Alfred Richards—through which he made the first attempt to organise the workers. Towards the end of 1919, the economic depression grew worse and many of these workers, who happened to be waterfront workers, began clamouring for higher wages and better conditions. The employers refused. Cipriani put his organisation to the test. He called on the waterfront workers to lay down their tools. The men stopped work immediately and at Cipriani's request

CAPT. A.A. CIPRIANI AT A LABOUR MEETING

demonstrated in the street. There was no settlement of the dispute for days, and on 22 December, 1919, the men marched through the business section of the city ordering shops to close down. Through fright, most of the shop-owners obeyed at once. A newspaper report of the next day said: "Messrs. Fogarty and Stephens Limited did not immediately comply, but resistance was not long before the doors were run over."

And the resistance of the employers was not long either, thanks to the effort of Captain Cipriani in organising the workers.

Because of the event, the government of Trinidad and Tobago (which at the time was clearly sympathising with the employers) enacted and passed this country's first Strike Ordinance. Its action was swift, too, for the date of the passing of this Ordinance was 13 January, 1920, hardly a month after the Christmas incidents.

But this did not stop the workers, now alert to their strength and to their rights. With the growth of the oil industry throughout the 1920s and 1930s, industrial disputes grew more prevalent, and the situation gave rise to the emergence of labour leader Uriah Butler, and to the widely-known oilfield riots of 1937. This latter event, which resulted from a strike, changed Trinidad's industrial affairs for all times. So it is good to call to mind the strike of November 1919, the first industrial strike in Trinidad.

FORTYFOUR
CHAPTER

THE FIRST GENERAL ELECTION (1925)

W hen day dawned on Saturday, 7 February, 1925, it was, politically speaking, the most eventful occasion the country had seen up to that time.

The labour of all the years had at last borne fruit. Despite all that had gone before—the reform upheaval of the 1880s, the unsympathetic Franchise Commission of 1888, the suspension of the Borough Council of Port-of-Spain in 1899, the Red House Fire in 1903; and through the decades, the ceaseless agitation of men like Mzumbo Lazare, Edgar Maresse-Smith, Cyrus Prudhomme David, Alfred Richards, as well as the returned soldiers from the First World War, especially the returned soldier Captain Andrew Cipriani—despite all this—it was only now that the people of Trinidad and Tobago were having their first General Elections.

It was a great thrill that the day had finally come. Those who had fought for reform were overjoyed. Although they did not get the unlimited franchise that they desired, they may have felt that they had a lot to be grateful for. They may have thought mainly of Major E. L .F. Wood whom the British had sent to lead a Commission here in 1921, because of the agitation for reform. Major Wood had recommended that only seven out of 26 seats should be elected by the people, and although this was far from being good enough, the people were glad that they had at least got something.

The authorities had divided the country into seven seats, which were the following: Port-of-Spain, St. Andrew-Nariva-Mayaro, Victoria, St. Patrick, St. George, Caroni and Tobago.

The seats of County Victoria and St. Andrew-Nariva-Mayaro were decided in special elections earlier that year: Victoria on 20 January, when T. M. Kelshall was victor; and St. Andrew-Nariva-Mayaro on 17 January, when Charles Henry Pierre was victor.

Of the five seats to be elected on that historic day, 7 February, 1925, the one drawing most attention was Port-of-Spain, not merely because Port-of-Spain was the capital, but because one of the men contesting the seat had become a legend in the land. This man was Captain Cipriani. The masses were clamouring for him, but the masses as such could not vote, for the franchise was limited to the property-owning class. Cipriani's opponents in the elections were the oil pioneer Randolph Rust and barrister Gaston Johnston.

Election Day was like Carnival in Port-of-Spain, with crowds milling round the main polling station, the Town Hall, and with bands of people on truck and on foot shouting out calypsoes and parading Cipriani colours up and down Knox Street and Frederick Street. Many lorries passed by with string-bands and festooned with flags and buntings and with people crying out the name of Cipriani in the street.

Randolph Rust's supporters were also very much in evidence, but much more subdued, while there was comparatively little of Gaston Johnston.

At the end of the day, Cipriani's supporters were in ecstasy because the Captain crushed his opponents, polling 2,557 votes to Randolph Rust's 910. Gaston Johnston trailed with 378.

In county St. George, the proprietor and agriculturist Albert Victor Stollmeyer triumphed over A. Cory Davies to win the seat in the Legislative Council, while in St. Patrick the victor was E. Radcliffe Clarke. The St. Patrick victory gave an idea of how confined was the electorate, for in this large county Radcliffe Clarke won with only 314 votes against his opponent, A. A. Sobrian, who polled 269.

The seat for county Caroni went to Sarran Teelucksingh, who was at the time one of the most popular men in the region. He won from the agriculturist and sugar planter Ernest Robinson, polling 491 votes to Robinson's 235.

The fifth seat, Tobago, was taken by James Alexander Biggart.

So the electoral scoreboard read: Port-of-Spain—Captain Andrew Cipriani; St. Andrew-Nariva-Mayaro—Charles Henry Pierre; Victoria—T.M. Kelshall; St. Patrick—E. Radcliffe Clarke; St. George—Albert Victor Stollmeyer; Caroni—Sarran Teelucksingh; Tobago—James Alexander Biggart.

These were the first General Elections in Trinidad and Tobago, and the historic day was 7 February, 1925.

CHAPTER FORTYFIVE

THE FIRST AIRMAIL SERVICE (1929)

T he first letters ever to come to Trinidad by air arrived just around 6 p.m. on Sunday, 22 September, 1929. The 16 years which had separated this event from the ill-starred event of 23 January, 1913, were 16 years of stunning development for the flying machine—now commonly known as the aeroplane.

It will be recalled that on that day in January 1913, the American aviator Frank Boland had crashed to his death after lifting off from the Queen's Park Savannah and spending just about two minutes in the air. A month later, George Schmitt arrived and revelled in success, but had spent no more than 10 minutes in the air, making five laps of the Savannah, and attaining a maximum height of just over 3,000 feet. Of course these statistics were wildly amazing in 1913—unbelievable—and in 1929, they already had the flavour of a joke.

Man had not only gone up many thousands of feet into the air, and stayed hours, but had already crossed the Atlantic in the flying machine. And this island of Trinidad, always in close contact with the amazing developments of the world, had the honour of seeing that same man who had made the Atlantic crossing for the first time in the world. The man was Charles Lindbergh, and he had covered himself with glory by flying in the machine from New York to Paris alone and non-stop. This had occurred two years before—in 1927. Soon afterwards it was shown that there was enough confidence in air travel for the world's first airline to be set up—Pan American Airways. The company was using what was called "amphibian" planes, planes that came to rest on water—for landing on the ground still had its great problems.

In 1929 the new company, Pan American Airways, boldly decided to inaugurate an airmail service to South America, with a scheduled stop at Trinidad. When the announcement was made early that year, 1929, excitement ran high, but when the actual moment came, the impact on Trinidad could hardly be described. Thousands of people had thronged the Port-of-Spain waterfront, waiting to welcome the great Lindbergh, and as the time due for his arrival came, 5.45 p.m., they looked towards the hills tensely. Pan American was on time from the start, for a reporter on the scene wrote: "At 5.45 exactly the cry went up, 'Look him there!' and a murmuring which grew in volume until it spread for miles, was heard, and gradually the airliner was seen to glide over the mountains like a large bird, and headed for Port-of-Spain."

Coming over the northern hills, Lindbergh was aware what warmth and admiration lay below, and he decided to give the onlookers a treat. He came in flying low, circled over Port-of-Spain and then headed straight for the Bocas, turned back and headed for the lane leading to his base. It must have been a wonderful sight. He touched the water, said the reporter, as gracefully as a heron, and taxied up to the anchorage. This landing base of Pan American was just off the customs wharf. Several officials left the wharf in a launch, and soon at the anchorage were the aide-de-camp for the Acting Governor, as well as a special representative of Pan American Airways, the Commandant of the Local Forces, G.H. May; and, of course, the Post-Master General, Burnley Littlepage. There was certainly a photographer there, also, for Lindbergh was pictured handing a bag of mail to Littlepage. In all, Lindberg brought eight packages of mail.

However, amidst the historic celebrations, there was another point to look at. The thousands of people who had come in from all parts of the country were kept waiting to see Lindbergh, while dusk fell rapidly. In fact, it was 7.15, when they could see nothing, that Lindbergh was eventually free from the customs to come ashore. He came ashore with his wife beside him, the brave lady who herself could fly the plane, and who had at that time and later written so much about the advances in air travel. Lindbergh came ashore to thunderous cheers, for the people did not budge, but waited to see him—of course only a few managed that. Lindbergh later complained bitterly about being detained at the customs so long after a tiring flight.

However, he gave an idea of coming events when he told a reporter: "It is customary that when we open new routes to first carry airmail, and when we get things going we open for passengers." The first of the passengers—three of them—were to be brought here by pilot J.H. Tilton in 1930. It is, however, not Tilton we are concerned with now, nor with the first passengers to come here, nor indeed the advances in air travel. We are concerned with the bright and historic evening of Sunday, 22 September, 1929, when Charles Lindbergh brought eight packages of mail to Trinidad by air, thus giving Trinidad an airmail service for the first time.

CHAPTER FORTY SIX

THE FIRST AIRMAN OF TRINIDAD (1934)

T he most wildly popular and the most versatile sporting hero Trinidad has ever known became in his later years Trinidad's first airman. Perhaps it could be said that he has been Trinidad's only airman, in the sense that he owned and flew his own airplane. This man was Mikey Cipriani, one of the most amazing figures in Trinidad's history.

Mikey, who was born in 1890, was, with Lebrun Constantine, the first great sporting hero of this country. He emerged early, and as a teenager dominated most of the field of outdoor sports, especially cycling. Cycling was to him a passion, and on the days of big cycle and athletic sports, held at that time by the Queen's Park Cricket Club at the Queen's Park Oval in Port-of-Spain, the crowds who rushed to see Mikey Cipriani ride were never disappointed. At various times he beat all the best cyclists in the Caribbean, and in 1910, at championship games in Port-of-Spain, he crowned himself champion cyclist of the West Indies.

He was, in addition, one of the foremost cricketers in the land, and represented Trinidad in Barbados in 1911. He was also regarded as brilliant at football, one of the main problems here being that "he could play in any position", so that the captain did often not know where to place him. Added to this, he was a pole-vaulter of exceptional ability, as well as a fine boxer.

But the clouds of war swept over all this, for when, on 4 August, 1914, the First World War broke out, Mikey Cipriani put aside his racing bicycle, his cricket and football gear, the vaulting pole and boxing gloves, and headed for Europe. He did not sail with the Trinidad contingent that left that year, but so far as it is known, went privately. He joined the Second Life Guards and was sent to the fighting front in France, and there he contended with the crack of rifles and sweaty trenches. In that interlude he had something of a charmed life, escaping death a number of times. For instance, at the famous Battle of Mons, the Germans wiped out an entire allied battalion, leaving only a few survivors. Mikey was one of those. He had fought so heroically that he was later decorated with the Medal of Mons.

He came home again when the war was over in 1918, and the sporting crowd clamoured for him once again. But he was already 29, and not the same sporting figure they had known. He entered the annual Cycle and Athletic Sports at the Queen's Park Oval in 1921, but the magical prowess had vanished. Mikey Cipriani never raced again.

He gave up sports altogether, but although he was bent on carrying out his profession—he had studied law—he was not the man to settle down and remain quietly out of the limelight. What he chose now was a field of activity that was to make and break his life.

During the war he had seen the heavy flying machines pass over the trenches and he had become deeply fascinated with them. After he had returned home, he got married, and his wife went up to England on a holiday. One of her cousins there was at the time working for Geoffrey de Havilland—a man then pioneering the design and production of aircraft. When she wrote home telling about air-rides she was getting, Mikey quickly went up to England, not merely to be taken up into the air, too, but to see if he could learn to fly. He took flying lessons, learned to fly a plane in record time, and before returning to Trinidad, ordered his own aircraft from de Havilland.

Apparently, the airplane was shipped to Trinidad, and a friend of his, the aviator Earle Lickfold, conducted pleasure flights for a time, using the old runway on the Piarco Savannah. That runway had been laid down by a French pioneer airline, Compagnie Générale Aeropostale, that plied between France and South America. It is said that Mikey dug up that strip and laid down what he saw as a proper runway, but this is disputed sometimes. This particular area is today the site of Piarco Airport.

Despite the novelty and the glitter of air travel, the Piarco Savannah was very remote in those days, and the joy rides there did not attract many customers.

Mikey was flying the plane now, and, together with his wife, journeyed to the Piarco Savannah every evening. In the little two-seater plane, which they called "Hummingbird", they explored the surrounding airspace.

It was not long before Mikey Cipriani journeyed beyond the island and before his fame as a flier began to spread. As the 1930s approached he flew to Grenada—where he was entertained by the governor—and later he received the same reception in Barbados and St. Vincent.

His fame was now even greater and even more widespread than in the early days. The "Hummingbird" was a familiar sight in the skies of Trinidad, and indeed in the skies of Tobago. However, he could not land in Tobago as there was no runway there. Excited crowds were always out in the streets watching him and daring him to land.

A few years later there came a great moment in his life. The date was 22 October, 1933, and the dirigible, Graf Zeppelin, on its way to Germany from South America, flew low over Trinidad. It came in at half-past five in the morning and great crowds got up to see it, and they waved and cheered all along its route. It came in from the south-east, over Mayaro, as day dawned, and it travelled in a diagonal direction towards Port-of-Spain. It flew so low that all along the route people rushed out to wave to its occupants. When it got to Port-of-Spain it descended even lower, dropping from 500 feet to 200 feet. It was now about six o'clock in Port-of-Spain and all over the city people were shouting themselves hoarse, greeting the wonderful apparition in the sky.

Making most of this spectacular situation, Mikey Cipriani went up to meet the Graf Zeppelin. He encountered it before it reached the city and escorted it into Port-of-Spain. To many who saw the two crafts coming in, Mikey's "Hummingbird" circling the Graf Zeppelin was like a mosquito circling a whale.

Following this, the crucial moment came for Mikey Cipriani. He was at the height of his career and in the full brightness of his fame as an airman, but none could have guessed what lay beyond the horizon. At the beginning of 1934, the government of Trinidad and Tobago, eager to create an air link between the two islands, called on Mikey Cipriani to chart a route. At this point, air flight was becoming common, and it was clear that Tobago was little more than half-an-hour away by air, while it was nine weary hours by sea. So they put the matter into the hands of Mikey Cipriani.

Mikey himself was anxious to have that Tobago route established, and to start, he had to have a landing strip in Tobago. This was soon looked after. The authorities built a suitable runway for "Hummingbird" at Shirvan Park.

On the morning of Sunday, 3 June, 1934, Mikey Cipriani set out to make his first-ever landing in Tobago. His wife could not go with him that day, and to accompany him went his friend, Leslie Bradshaw, one of the well-known footballers in Port-of-Spain. Mikey and Leslie set off with offcial documents, it is believed, the day's newspapers, and several messages, and they took off and disappeared into the hazy skies towards the northern hills. Thousands of eyes watched the little plane melt into the distance. The arrangement was that as soon as Mikey reached Tobago he would telephone his wife.

But the message never came. Mikey's wife, as well as the authorities, waited patiently, then nervously, then in the case of Mikey's wife, hysterically, but the telephone never rang. On that bright and historic morning of 3 June, 1934, disaster was in the air. Mikey Cipriani was lost.

As soon as the news broke that Mikey Cipriani was overdue in Tobago and could not be accounted for, volunteer searchers set off for the forests of the northern range. The whole country was plunged into gloom.

Several groups of volunteers, including boy scouts and girl guides, went into the forests every day, looking for signs of the wreckage of the

TROOPER MIKEY CIPRIANI
KING'S HOUSEHOLD BATTALION IN WORLD WAR I.

"Hummingbird," but it was only eight days after the crash, on Monday, 11 June, 1934, that it was found. The remains of the "Hummingbird" and of the two fliers were brought back to Port-of-Spain that evening.

The funeral of Mikey Cipriani was one of the most spectacular Port-of-Spain had ever seen, judging from the public demonstration of grief that followed the cortege, the crowds of onlookers who lined the streets, and the tumult that took place inside the cemetery.

Mikey was buried at Mucurapo Cemetery, not far across the road from where he had set off on his fateful trip. More than 20,000 people witnessed the burial—and this number was about a third of Port-of-Spain's population at that time. The date was Tuesday, 12 June, 1934, and it was the close of the short, bright history of the first airman that Trinidad ever knew.

CHAPTER FORTY SEVEN

SOUND RADIO COMES TO TRINIDAD (1935)

T he first time that sound radio made an impact in Trinidad was in 1934, when calypsonians Lion and Attila, who had gone on tour to the United States of America, did a broadcast of calypsoes back to Trinidad.

News of the fact that they were to do this broadcast caused great stir in Port-of-Spain, and on the appointed night, 8 March, 1934, people crowded the streets of Port-of-Spain in front of the few houses with radio in order to listen to these calypsonians. The broadcast, which was over a station called W2XAF, proved to be a disappointment, because it was so inaudible. All that could be heard was the faint voice of Lion singing his well-known: "Bad woman, oh, oh, oh!"

However, shortly after this experience came the first broadcast which was successfully heard in Trinidad. The broadcast was transmitted from an experimental shortwave radio station in Barbados, and the occasion was the 1935 cricket series between the Marylebone Cricket Club (MCC) and the West Indies, played at Kensington Oval, Barbados. A more exciting match could not have been chosen for this broadcast which, incidentally, was the first ball-by-ball cricket commentary to be heard here. There were startling declarations in the match and neither side scored more than 102 runs in an inning. And in the end the MCC won. Seen from another point of view, it was really radio that won. Never before were Trinidad crowds thrown into the heat of excitement by a match taking place outside of this island.

But that very 1935 MCC tour was to provide more startling occurrences in radio, so far as Trinidad was concerned. On January 18, in that year, 1935, readers saw the Trinidad Guardian banner headline: TRINIDAD GOES ON AIR FOR THE FIRST TIME. The newspaper's report declared: "The first officially approved broadcast of the match between Trinidad and the MCC team was transmitted yesterday by Mr. Diego Serrao, the Trinidad amateur and radio expert, who has set up his own broadcasting station in his home . . . Yesterday he gave the latest scores at regular intervals and provided a concert of grammophone records when he was not broadcasting."

Mr. Serrao's broadcasting station was upstairs in a house on Elizabeth Street overlooking the Queen's Park Oval cricket pitch. There, perched on the balcony with his electrical gadgets, he must have had an excellent view of play.

Developments in radio were taking place with amazing speed. For example, while just one year before, on 8 March, 1934, the calypsonians Lion and Attila could not have been heard clearly when they broadcast from New York, in February 1935, following Mr. Serrao's performance, crowds were able to listen comfortably to another New York broadcast, now from Attila, Beginner, and Tiger.

The next year, 1936, brought another significant moment. Radio sets were still expensive, and radio reception still far from perfect. Now a company calling itself Trinidad Radio Distribution set up a system to re-diffuse radio broadcasts coming from abroad. They felt that by "capturing" the broadcasts and re-transmitting them through a form of wired radio, they could eliminate reception interferences and thus make the broadcast more attractive to listen to. They planned to supply cheap receiving sets for homes to receive the programmes.

The company set up a powerful transmitter on Mount Hololo in Cascade and ran land lines all over the city. The work was completed in January 1936, and the first Re-Diffusion broadcast was made on 1

February, 1936. This happened to be the period when World Boxing Champion Joe Louis was achieving extraordinary fame, and his ring exploits were thrilling the people of Trinidad.

After the establishment of Re-Diffusion, the next big occurrence was eleven years later, by which time radio itself was no longer a novelty. Yet it was a significant event. True, since 1943 people had been listening to regular radio broadcasts coming from Port-of-Spain, but this was from the American Forces Radio (Station WVDI) and was not local in the true sense of the word.

But in 1947 Trinidad was ready for its own radio station, and on 31 August that year, a new company called the Trinidad Broadcasting Company Limited, headed by William McLurg, and with headquarters at 11B Maraval Road, inaugurated the station "Radio Trinidad".

On that first night, Governor Sir John Shaw did the official opening, and the programme included a memorable getting together of local artistes and musicians. There was also the programme, This is Trinidad, described as "a picture in sound and words", describing this country.

At that point, Re-Diffusion was still there, as indeed it is today. It seemed good value in 1947 with a rental of $2.00 a month for the receiving sets, and with 14 hours of broadcasting a day.

Yet, it is not Re-diffusion, nor Radio Trinidad, upon which emphasis is placed now. The one singled out is Mr. Diego Serrao, who, perched on the balcony of that house in Elizabeth Street, made history. The calendar was showing the date "17 January, 1935" when, with his radio gadgets, and overlooking the field of play from a house near to the Queen's Park Oval, he broadcast the game, and put Trinidad on the air for the first time.

CHAPTER FORTYEIGHT

THE FIRST VESSEL TO COME ALONGSIDE AT THE WATERFRONT (1939)

B efore the year 1935, Port-of-Spain did not have a deep-water harbour, and ships had to remain some distance out in the Gulf. Whatever merchandise or passengers they brought had to come to the wharf by means of small boats and lighters.

This also applied to anything going out to the ships. In that year, 1935, a move was made to provide Port-of-Spain with a deep-water harbour, which would have a great significance for trade and tourism, for it would make a great deal of difference when a ship could just come up to the wharf and anchor alongside.

The first ship to come alongside in Port-of-Spain was the "Governor", and it was a great moment to see the vessel, guided by tugs, settle itself, and cast anchor alongside the wharf. The day was Sunday, 16 March, 1939.

It was also a great moment for the authorities, for this marked the end of a long struggle with the owner of a fleet of lighters, a man of great influence in high places who did not want to see a deep-water harbour in Trinidad. This man was so powerful that he kept the government at bay for several years, until at long last, in April 1934, the Chamber of Commerce voted in favour of a deep-water harbour. The Secretary of State for the Colonies recommended a loan of £1,000,000 (then nearly $5,000,000), which was the estimated cost of the project, and construction of the deep-water harbour began on 6 March, 1935. On that date, workmen started to build a retaining wall from a point adjacent to the Mucurapo River off Wrightson Road. This was the first step for the reclaiming of land from the sea.

The deep-water harbour project was up to that time by far the biggest project ever undertaken in Trinidad, and it was about to drastically change the south-western face of Port-of-Spain. There had to be a great amount of land reclamation, since the waterfront, very shallow in parts, had to be extended to meet deep water. And of course the harbour had to be elaborately dredged to provide an approach channel.

The effect of the project was going to be a great deal more than merely providing Port-of-Spain with a deep-water harbour. One of the things it was going to do was to put to death the old, quaint, but ramshackle and insanitary fishing village of Corbeau Town, for not only the people, but the corbeaux would soon find themselves without a beach. The project would also cause the removal of revered landmarks such as the picturesque fish market at Corbeau Town, which was perched on the edge of a long jetty. This would be gone by 1937.

What would also go would be the crab-infested (and no doubt germ-infested) mangroves, so beloved and so much frequented by the little boys of Woodbrook. These mangroves lay on the side of the sea, off a little roadway called Wrightson Road. At least that part of the town had remained very much as it had been when Walsh Wrightson had built the roadway in 1900. But all this would change soon. As the work progressed, one of the firms that would be left 'high and dry' would be one of the oldest firms in Port-of-Spain, the Trinidad Trading Company. (This firm had been registered in 1921 as the Trinidad Shipping and Trading Company.)

The quay wall was to run in a straight line from in front of the Mucurapo Pumping Station to the tip of the St. Vincent Street jetty. The line of wall in relation to the coast was like a string to a bow. All the sea between the bow-string and the land had to be reclaimed. The work went on steadily from April 1935 until all the reclamation was completed.

The reclaimed area was so vast that the authorities could not leave it bare, and also, since Wrightson Road had begun from the western end of London Street to lead to the Mucurapo Pump House, it was desirable for an access road to be made from the south-eastern end of Wrightson Road and right across the reclaimed lands to Marine Square and South Quay. So the authorities decided to extend Wrightson Road.

It was then that the brilliant young engineer, Ranjit Kumar, came into the picture. While the deep-water harbour works were still going on, Ranjit, with his area of operation already reclaimed and settled began the great work. However, in 1939 he had to stop abruptly. He had already finished the south-eastern stretch, ending at the junction of St. Vincent Street and South Quay, and he had turned toward extending the north-western end, in order to take it some distance further, into Mucurapo Road. However, when war broke out in August 1939, all major public works had to stop, and Ranjit had to desist. He had reached as far west as Petra Street in Woodbrook.

It was a good thing for Port-of-Spain that the deep-water harbour had already been completed. It had taken more than three years to build the quay wall for the work which had begun in April 1935 was finished in October 1938. With the building of the wall, reclamation had been going on, and by October 1938 also, the reclamation was complete—or very nearly so. Facilities for shipping were established and as was said, on Sunday, 16 February, 1939, the deep-water harbour welcomed its first ship alongside: the "Governor", which was a merchant vessel of 3,495 tons, drawing nearly 27 feet of water. The man who piloted the ship alongside was a Trinidadian, Prince Conelly, and a newspaper report said of his effort: "Nearing her moorings she turned easily and slipped quietly into place, to the delight of the crowd assembled there."

That day the "Governor" took on 7,000 tons of sugar bound for Europe. And so it is with sweet memories we recall, no only 16 February, 1939, when it all ended, but that day in April 1935, when it all began, for it was on that day that the move was made to give Port-of-Spain a deep-water harbour for the first time.

CHAPTER FORTYNINE

T H E   F I R S T   H I G H W A Y   (1 9 4 2)

T he first highway in Trinidad was built by the American forces who came to this country in 1941.

Immediately after they had arrived here, for the purpose of setting up bases in Trinidad, they got on with the task of erecting the two bases for the defence of the area—the naval base at Chaguaramas, and the army air base at Cumuto. In the meantime, they began developing docks in Port-of-Spain in order to bring in heavy equipment. The Port-of-Spain deep-water harbour had just been completed, and the Americans were developing the Woodbrook end of the harbour, an area they called Docksite.

Naturally, the Americans wished to have quick and easy communication with these three military points, as well as with their Base Command, which was at Whitehall. It was impossible, however, to have such communication by using the Eastern Main Road, for this road, apart from having traffic of its own, was narrow and often congested. In fact, in the early months of 1941, long convoys of American military vehicles were usually held up on this strip of road, which was of course the only link between Port-of-Spain and places east of it, like Cumuto. So they saw the need to construct their own road to connect their Cumuto Base—which they named Fort Read—

with Port-of-Spain. By December 1941, they announced that they were in the process of building such a road.

Just at this time, December 1941, the government's Morvant housing project was completed. It was rather isolated; no proper roads linked it to Port-of-Spain. Now following hard on the American announcement was one coming from the Government Housing Commissioner, Robert Grenfell, declaring that government was building a road through the Morvant township and over the Laventille hills. Grenfell said that the road was to continue beyond the housing project to link up "with the United States Army road to Cumuto".

This project soon started, and the governor of the day, Sir Hubert Young, actually landscaped part of that road, designing the "Look-out" so popular today. On completion, Grenfell named the road "Lady Young Road" after the governor's wife.

The Americans worked untiringly on building the Churchill-Roosevelt Highway, and a common sight on that strip was the bustling activity of bull-dozers and soldiers bare-backed in the sun. The road began about three miles south-east of the town of Arima and ended at a point at the western extremity of Barataria, forming a junction with the Eastern Main Road.

With the American soldiers working at top speed to finish this road, its progress was amazingly fast, so much so that in early 1942 the Government's Information Officer, Wilson Minshall, could write: "The new Churchill-Roosevelt Highway has swept across country from a point near Laventille with the force of a flood rushing into a quiet valley. Cleared and graded but not yet surfaced, its naked earth weaves and interweaves protesting patterns under the wheels of army trucks and construction tractors that cannot wait till the road is finished . . ."

The fact that they could not wait until the road was finished showed how urgently such a road was needed. The road was soon finished, and it was opened on 17 May, 1942. It was seen to be a beautiful, well-constructed highway, although it was done in such haste, and it stood out as being the only roadway of this sort in Trinidad. Apart from the way it was constructed, what was so different about it was that it was completely free from settlements along its

FIRST IN TRINIDAD

route, a factor which was bound to help in the quick and free transit of vehicles.

But what must be borne in mind is that it was not a public road, and also, under the American Leased Bases Agreement, it had nothing to do with the government of Trinidad and Tobago. It was a completely military strip, constructed by the Americans for their own use, and it needs not be said that the Trinidad public was not allowed to use it. From the time it was opened in 1942 up to the end of the war in 1945, the Churchill-Roosevelt Highway was a strictly military, and it was not until much later that it was handed over to the Trinidad and Tobago government.

The Churchill-Roosevelt Highway has undergone radical changes since the Americans built it, and indeed if one of those Americans who helped to build the highway in 1942 were to come back to the area he certainly would not recognise the road. In the 1980s, the entire western section from about the region of Tacarigua was transformed, and the rest of the road up to the old Fort Read itself underwent the same development.

The highway area of the old base, Fort Read, might remain the same for a long time to come, and this area, with the heavy concrete columns at its entry, might be the only thing that reminds of the American days.

At the sight of these columns those of us who are old enough, and who have seen, might remember those early days of 1942, when American army equipment and American soldiers, bare-backed in the sun, were constructing the Churchill-Roosevelt Highway, the first highway in Trinidad.

The Americans did not think of any local figures in considering a name for their highway. What was firing their minds was the mid-Atlantic Conference between the American President Franklin Delano Roosevelt and British Prime Minister Winston Churchill which had taken place in August 1941. That was the conference that had drawn America into the war. It had led directly to the Leased Bases Agreement with Trinidad and Tobago, and was therefore responsible for the building of that road. So what would they call the road? It was

157

so obvious to them that they must have felt that the road named itself. That was why from the very start they called it the "Churchill Roosevelt Highway".

CHAPTER FIFTY

THE FIRST TIME THE STEELBANDS CAME OUT ONTO THE STREET (1945)

THE FIRST TIME THE STEELBANDS CAME OUT ONTO THE STREET (1945)

The first time in Trinidad that the steelbands came out onto the streets was on Tuesday, 8 May, 1945, in the heat and joyous wildness of V-E Day.

V-E Day was the day that the Allied Victory in Europe was celebrated. It was the day after the German surrender, when the Second World War came to a close in Europe. Actually two days for celebration were given, Tuesday and Wednesday, 8 and 9 May, 1945.

The steelband as we know it today was in its infancy then, and the tunes it could play were very elementary ones like "Mary had a little lamb", and a popular four-note tune the name of which came from an advertisement: "Alan Ladd—This Gun For Hire".

Just before that time, two youths discovered that notes could be got on the pans by subjecting them to heat and shaping them out with the use of a hammer.

Possibly, many others had realised this at the time, but certainly, the youths, Winston Simon, of a band called *John-John* (later *Tokyo*), and Ellie Manette, of a band called *Oval Boys* (later *Invaders*) were two of the pioneers of steelband melody. Winston was only 15 in 1945, and Ellie about 17.

The steelband, which must have evolved from the tamboo-bamboo and bottle-and-spoon forms of music of the 1930s and before, was by the early 1940s deemed a nuisance. In those times of acute unemployment and hardship, which was due mainly to the war in Europe, young men grouped together and sought to have fun by banging on oil drums. This was a marked phenomenon in Port-of-Spain, and to some extent, in San Fernando.

What complicated matters and hardened feelings against these rhythm-makers was the fact that the people who were involved with the steelband were the young men who crowded the courts every day, answering to charges of robbery with violence, riotous behaviour, hooliganism, and matters of the sort. Such a high incidence of these things took place in the early years of the 1940s that the government was forced to re-introduce whipping, by means of the "cat-o-nine tails", in an effort to check crime.

Steelband and its followers were associated with crime and violence, and, in general, an undesirable way of life, and so no one with any claim to respectability would have been seen to take any interest in the steelband. At times the steelband beaters would attempt to beat their pans on the streets, but this always resulted in arrests, rough-handling by the police, and in seizures of pans.

An anti-noise law, aimed at prohibiting the steelband once and for all times, was being contemplated just around the time that the historic day arrived—Tuesday, 8 May, 1945. At 9 a.m. that morning British Prime Minister Winston Churchill announced the German surrender which released such unbridled joy in Trinidad that everyone came out onto the street in wild jubilation. It was spontaneous Carnival, with crowds forming bands right there on the streets after the announcement. Of course the steelbands had come out to celebrate too, and the people, attracted by the infectious, pulsating rhythm, joined with the steelband to make the celebrations of the victory in Europe the most extraordinary that Port-of-Spain had seen up to that time.

Although the crowds were shouting out King Radio's "All day, all night, Mary Ann", the road march of the time, everyone must have

AN EARLY STEELBAND

paid attention to the steelband. People were amazed that it could produce such wonderful rhythm, and could actually play a few musical notes.

For those two whole days and nights, up to midnight on Wednesday, the steelbands and the crowds roamed the streets in joyous celebration, and that was certainly the occasion that led to the overwhelming popularity of the steelband in Trinidad.

However, the authorities were not fully convinced, for the anti-noise bill was passed in December 1945. Yet, those wonderful V-E days were the start of the road to recognition and to glory, and they marked, apart from the end of the war, a distinct historic movement—the movement when the steelbands came out onto the streets for the first time.

CHAPTER FIFTYONE

THE FIRST ADULT FRANCHISE ELECTIONS (1946)

Although as many as 21 years separated the first general elections from the first adult franchise elections, in terms of seats to be fought for it had meant an addition of only two.

In the first general elections, which took place in 1925, there were only seven seats to be elected, while in the first adult franchise elections to take place in 1946, there were nine. Yet, on closer examination, it was a greater advance than at first appeared. In 1925, the seven seats conceded were out of a full house of 26, whereas in 1946, the nine seats were out of a full house of 18. In 1946, people were going to the polls to elect half of the Legislative Council.

Seven seats were what had been recommended by the Wood Commission of 1921, and which were established at the elections of 1925. The two additional seats in the 1946 elections came about because Port-of-Spain was divided into two constituencies—North Port-of-Spain and South Port-of-Spain, which yielded one additional seat. The other came about because, while in 1925 the geographical county Victoria was considered one seat, by 1946 San Fernando had grown to such an extent that it was decided to make the town a separate constituency.

The day of the historic first adult franchise elections was Monday, 1 July, 1946, and as if to show that this day was different from other ordinary days, wild torrential rains swept the country. The hostile weather served not just to set apart the day, but to keep voters all over the country from going to the polls. This could be seen by the fact that out of a total electorate of 257,318 persons in 1946, only 117,000 votes were cast.

But the weather was not the only factor in this low poll. There were thousands of spoilt votes, which may have been the result of the great illiteracy which prevailed at that time. And, of course, ignorance of voting procedures was a great problem, too, this being the first time that the ordinary man in Trinidad and Tobago was facing the ballot box.

The Port-of-Spain seat attracted special notice, as could be imagined. What made it special at these elections were the contestants for the constituency of North Port-of-Spain. Because here, the anointed of the oil belt, Uriah Butler, had chosen to leave his happy hunting ground of St. Patrick to try to dethrone the popular Albert Gomes. The South Port-of-Spain constituency also had unusual interest. In this seat, a young doctor called Patrick Solomon was pitting his strength against one of the most experienced men in the social and political affairs of this country: Alfred Richards, whose name was now a byword. He had established what became the first political party in Trinidad, but which, at its founding in 1896-1897, was more like a trade union than a political pressure-group. In 1946, Alfred Richards was already in his 80s.

But first to consider what happened in North Port-of-Spain. Butler, still with the aura of a hero because of the oilfield riots of 1937, was dealt a crushing defeat at the polls. Gomes received 5,172 votes while Butler received only 2,018.

In South Port-of-Spain, Dr. Patrick Solomon, who belonged to a bright new, radical party, the United Front, defeated Alfred Richards, polling 4,239 votes to only 1,357 for Richards.

For the St. George seat, three new faces were contesting honours: Mitra Sinanan, Norman Tang, and Chanka Maraj. Chanka Maraj was a Butler Party candidate, and in the constituency of St. George he profited much more from being in the Butler Party than Butler himself did in the constituency of North Port-of-Spain. For Chanka vanquished his opponents, polling 8,000 votes to the 6,000 polled by the second-place candidate, Mitra Sinanan.

Just south of St. George was county Caroni, and there an upset of a different nature took place. It was not so much a battle of parties, as of personalities. On the one hand was the almost legendary Sarran Teelucksingh, a man who had been in the Legislative Council since 1925, and a man whose tent cinemas had made him famous all around the country. On the other hand was Clarence Abidh, who had fought him twice before, unsuccessfully. Abidh had worked hard, hoping to achieve what seemed impossible. It was to be third time lucky for Clarence Abidh and he humiliated Teelucksingh, polling 7,123 to Teelucksingh's 2,020.

But it was in the constituency of Victoria that the most stunning electoral blow was delivered. And it was the height of irony that the only candidate who could have been considered a stranger to the public scattered his opponents with the biggest majority of the elections. This candidate was Ranjit Kumar who had come to Trinidad from India only a few years before. Nevertheless he appealed to the agricultural peasants of the vast, sugar-growing county of Victoria, for on election day, these people swept him into the Legislative Council, giving him a massive 13,220 votes—three times as many as the second place candidate, the trade inionist McDonald Moses.

As a contrast, San Fernando proved to be the simplest and most predictable seat of all. No one who knew the area and knew the candidate could have expected victory to go to anyone else but Roy Joseph. Here, it was personality and not party that carried the day. Roy, known and loved throughout San Fernando (especially by the women) for his chivalry and his friendly flamboyance, had the seat "reserved" for him from the time he entered the elections. It was a pity that the good and able Ralph Mentor, a trade union candidate, had to pit himself against the wildly popular Roy. On that depressingly wet day in San Fernando, Roy's supporters turned out to give this candidate a massive 6,000 votes (massive for such a small constituency) as against Mentor's 1,844 votes.

Perhaps the highest drama of the whole elections was provided by the fight for the St. Patrick seat, for here was where Uriah Butler was the anointed and for many the unshakeable. Butler had caused consternation by leaving this safe seat to fight Albert Gomes in Gomes' own "citadel" of North Port-of-Spain, and for many the chief had left St. Patrick "exposed." He had put Timothy Roodal there, and although Roodal was a veteran of many campaigns and not unloved, the general feeling was that his style was the style of the past and not suited for the elections of 1946—especially as his opponent was the clever, radical leader of the United Front Party, Jack Kelshall. Jack Kelshall, freshly home from the wars, was bringing a bright post-war message of change and deliverance, a message of hope for the quick end of the colonial days, and the promise of a place in the sun. Many of his supporters were claiming that he had made Uriah Butler run for cover. Everyone felt that Roodal was no match for Jack Kelshall. Yet Kelshall, far ahead of his time, made the mistake of calling for the "nationalising" of the oil industry, and this was what Roodal needed to swing his campaign. On election day, he crushed the enthusiastic Kelshall, polling 13,178, to Kelshall's 3,334.

The last seat in Trinidad was the biggest constituency of all, eastern counties, and here, too, it was the old order against the new. There was the figure of Vernon Wharton, khaki-clad, with breeches, leggings, and cork hat, reticent and severe, so reminiscent of the passing plantation times; and there was the young and dashing Victor Bryan, radical, like Kelshall, speaking of a new day, and even without speaking, the very clean-cut good-looking appearance of the man spoke volumes for brilliant times ahead.

Bryan, who came from Coal-mine, just off Sangre Grande, easily defeated Vernon Wharton. He polled 5,215 votes and Wharton, 749.

For the last seat, Tobago, we see another case of party swamping personality. There, the Member for Tobago in the Legislature, the widely-known racehorse owner George de Nobriga, was left standing at the gates. Humiliated, he received no more than 580 votes and lost his deposit. He was vanquished by the Butler candidate, A.P.T. James who topped 4,000 votes. The second-place candidate was L.E. Edwards who polled 1,625 votes.

THE RED HOUSE WAS PAINTED RED IN 1897 TO MARK QUEEN VICTORIA'S DIAMOND JUBILEE.

The nine men to represent the people of Trinidad and Tobago in the Legislative Council following the first adult franchise elections were:

Albert Gomes, representing North Port-of-Spain; Patrick Solomon, representing South Port-of-Spain; Chanka Maraj, representing St. George; Clarence Abidh, representing Caroni; Ranjit Kumar, representing Victoria; Roy Joseph, representing San Fernando; Timothy Roodal, representing St. Patrick; Victor Bryan, representing the Eastern Counties; and A.P.T. James, representing Tobago.

CHAPTER FIFTYTWO

THE FIRST INDEPENDENCE DAY (1962)

THE FIRST INDEPENDENCE DAY (1962)

T he first Independence Day of Trinidad and Tobago was chimed in at midnight on Friday, 31 August, 1962.

It was a night of spectacle and emotion in Port-of-Spain, and the emotion was heightened when, in the flood-lit fore-court of the Red House, the band of the Royal Marines struck up. Two tall flagpoles painted white were the main objects of attraction. On one of them the Union Jack slid slowly and gently down to the strains of "The Last Post", and afterwards on the other, rising and fluttering to the strains of "Forged from the Love of Liberty" was the red, black and white flag of Trinidad and Tobago.

("Forged from the Love of Liberty" was a new, specially-written work by Pat Castagne, and chosen as the National Anthem of Trinidad and Tobago.)

While this historic ceremony was taking place, the thousands of people standing in Knox Street, in Woodford Square and in other areas around the Red House, broke into thunderous applause. And it was no wonder, for it was the end of the long road to Independence—a road which started since early in 1888, when, as a result of a petition sent to Queen Victoria by the inhabitants of Fifth Company Village, Governor William Robinson appointed the first Royal Commission on

Franchise in Trinidad. (It is interesting to note the co-incidence that at that time Tobago had just entered the process of uniting with Trinidad. The first step towards uniting the two colonies was made in 1887, when the Trinidad and Tobago Act was promulgated, and the measure came into force from the first day of January, 1889.)

Along the way, the road to independence had, among its several landmarks, the limited general elections of 1925, the first adult franchise elections in 1946, the formation of the first party government and the advent of Eric Williams as chief minister in 1956, the coming of the first cabinet government in 1959, and the coming of full internal self-government in 1961.

And now the long sought Independence Day had arrived, the 31 August, 1962. There was indescribable joy and relief, especially from the men and women who had distinguished themselves in the early stages of the final thrust for independence, and who were there on that night.

Apart from Eric Williams himself, who had taken up the struggle in the early 1940s, there was Uriah Butler, whose campaign had gone back even further, to the beginning of the 1930s. Butler, who, as a labour leader, had sparked off the famous oilfield riots at Fyzabad in 1937, could have been said to have lit up the campaign in a way no one else had done. Butler, now a man of 69, was in a place of honour on this night.

Apart from the old campaigners, there was the man who had shot up like a star, from the lowest ranks of the civil service to the highest post in Trinidad and Tobago. This was Sir Solomon Hochoy, who was to be governor-general of the newly independent state. He had been knighted just a few months before.

On that glittering night of independence, the Princess Royal, representing Elizabeth II, the Queen of Great Britain and the Commonwealth, read a message handing over sovereignty and expressing confidence and goodwill. Then the chief minister of 1956, who had become premier when cabinet government came in 1959, and who with independence had automatically become prime minister, replied with gentle words. But the leader of the opposition,

Dr. Rudranath Capildeo, was not too overwhelmed to offer a terse word of warning. He said:

"It is fitting that at this historic moment independence is heralded with the adornment and lustre of British parliamentary democracy, and that it is dedicated to the British parliamentary tradition. Every such dedication is a barrier which evil minds will have to surmount in order to advance into totalitarian powers. The path of a new nation is paved with great temptation and dangers. Prejudice, always latent, could always become an instrument of policy. Means of information, the press and radio, by a calculated mixture of omission and distortion, are the complicated avant-guard in the destruction of democratic rule. And so democracy contains the germs of its own destruction, and tyranny could enshrine itself on the altar of popular rule. Nevertheless, we enter the future with high hopes."

Apart from the thousands of people in the square and around the Red House, representatives of 51 nations had come to Trinidad to witness the event, and as a result, the flags of 51 nations added splendour to the scene.

The moment of independence, which was heralded in by the Queen's message, by the raising of the national flag and the strains of the national anthem, by the chimes of church bells and the sirens of ships in the harbour, and by rockets and the flares all over the city, was a moment whose emotion can never be re-lived.

After the midnight independence ceremony, the crowds dispersed until later in the day when the Princess Royal opened the first sovereign Parliament of Trinidad and Tobago. She read the speech from the throne which, among other things, pledged the government to uphold democracy, guarantee freedom of worship, equality before the law, equality of opportunity in public employment, and to eliminate discrimination in private employment.

But perhaps the most impressive message of the entire independence celebrations was delivered the day before by Dr. Eric Williams. This was at a rally of school-children on the Queen's Park Oval. On the occasion Dr. Williams told the children: "Tomorrow, Independence Day, you will be the children of the independent state of

INDEPENDENCE DAY 1962: THE PRINCESS ROYAL INSPECTING THE PARADE.

Trinidad and Tobago. And in a few years after that you will be called upon by the law of the land to share in the privileges and responsibilities, the rights and duties of citizens. Tomorrow I shall have an equally great honour and responsibility: that of being the first prime minister of this independent nation. I am very happy therefore to take part in this memorable rally, and to send a message through you—the boys and girls here today at the Queen's Park Oval—to all the young people of Trinidad and Tobago."

The message was that the new nation must develop and maintain its political system, as well as its democratic machinery. It must provide the Members of Parliament, the doctors, lawyers, engineers, and artists. Dr. Williams added: "The nation is on the march. There is no turning back. The road from now on leads forward and only forward."

Those were stirring words to the young people. It was a message to serve as a beacon not only to the youth of the nation, but to everyone. However, when independence came a few hours later, all messages were drowned in emotion. It was a moment of joy and relief such as this country had never seen before.

CHAPTER FIFTYTHREE

THE FIRST TELEVISION SERVICE (1962)

elevision first came to Trinidad on Friday, 24 August, 1962, when television films, shot by Wilfred A. Lee and Company, commercial film producers of Park Street, Port-of-Spain, were transmitted by the newly-formed Trinidad and Tobago Television Company and shown on television sets here.

The films were of preparations for the first Independence Day celebrations.

However, the service only began months later. Trinidad and Tobago Television Company Limited was officially inaugurated on 1 November, 1962, when its studio was completed, and all preparations for tele-broadcasting fully made, and it was on that date that it began its service.

The company itself was formed towards the end of 1961. The majority shareholders were Re-Diffusion and Scottish Television, while the other shareholders were Columbia Broadcasting Systems and the Government of Trinidad and Tobago. The Company named as its first General Manager, Ronald Goodsman, and its first Board of Directors included Sir Patrick Hobson (Chairman), J.B. Dieffenthaler, Ken Ablack, Mark Jones, and Lord Brockhurst. The company had located premises at 11A Maraval Road, near the site of the old St. Clair

Women's Club, and work on the studio began in May 1962. Plans were pushed ahead with great speed for the express purpose of having arrangements completed before independence came, but this could not be realised. However, by the beginning of August 1962, arrangements were advanced enough to allow for a limited amount of transmission, and it was at this time that the firm of Wilfred A. Lee was commissioned to shoot independence material. The company had already appointed Ken Gordon as programme producer.

Shortly before 31 August came—Independence Day—the company announced that it would be televising the formal ceremony as well as parts of the celebrations, and 53 television sets were distributed in public places in the two big towns (40 in Port-of-Spain and 13 in San Fernando). As was stated above, the first transmission—a trial run— was made on Friday, 24 August, 1962.

That evening at 8 p.m. Trinidad and Tobago Television (TTT) began transmitting from its studios for the first time. It transmitted a bulletin of news on Channel 2, although some viewers were able to receive this on Channel 13.

The telecast was only partially successful, however.

The next big telecast began at 9 p.m. on 30 August, and the programme continued until this country's flag was raised, at midnight, bringing in Independence Day. Then, on Independence Day itself there was the telecasting of the proceedings in the Red House to the crowds in Woodford Square, and viewers were able to see the colourful ceremony in which Princess Royal read a speech of greetings from Queen Elizabeth II, and during which Prime Minister Dr. Eric Williams and Leader of the Opposition Rudranath Capildeo made brief addresses of reply.

But as was said, the official opening of the television service did not come until 1 November, 1962. At 6 p.m. on that Thursday, Acting Prime Minister Dr. Patrick Solomon declared the television station open. That evening the ceremony was telecast to about 1,000 homes.

Earlier that day, Television House was a hive of activity with rehearsals for the ceremony and final tests for the programme which was to follow afterwards. Among the items on the programme were "Television comes to Trinidad" and "Flying Doctor".

Since that occasion, great strides have been made in television the world over, and the next significant milestone here was when colour television was introduced in 1977. Despite the great technological advances that have come since, especially the instantaneous televising of events taking place in another part of the world (thanks to the use of satellites), we look back to what seem to be the infant days.

We recall the occasion at 7 p.m. on Friday, 24 August, 1962, when television pictures were seen in Trinidad for the first time.

CHAPTER FIFTYFOUR

OUR FIRST OLYMPIC CHAMPION (1976)

I n Montreal, the Olympic crowd was silent and tense as eight runners rose from their crouch to "set" position, and then the pistol cracked. Wild cheering and excitement broke out as the runners raced frantically down the lanes.

They were contending in the shortest Olympic distance, but at that moment, it must have seemed the longest in the world. As the runners crossed the half-way mark, one figure emerged from the bunch, and the screams and cries reached a wildness of frightening intensity. Soon, it was over. The athlete lunged, breasted the tape, and leapt into the air in jubilation. Warm applause resounded around the ground, but thousands of miles away in Trinidad it was not simply a question of warm applause, it was a question of incredible joy. People looking on in front of television sets broke into unrestrained cheering and celebration. The date was 24 July, 1976, and the athlete was Hasely Crawford from San Fernando. His victory meant the first Olympic gold medal for Trinidad and Tobago, and it set out Hasely as the first Olympic Champion this country has ever known.

Months later, at Carnival 1977, the calypsonian Maestro was to pay tribute with his song: "Gold! Gold! The fastest runner in the whole wide world!" and the Mighty Sparrow was to sing the infectious: "It's gold for Trinidad!"

Following the victory, that Olympic period was a season of great joy for Trinidad, and at the same time, the comparatively tiny dot on the world map that is this island must have become one of the biggest countries in the world on the map of world sport. People in distant parts of the world who heard of Trinidad for the first time must have asked themselves: Who is Hasely Crawford? But in Trinidad, this name had suddenly become the biggest in the land. On his arrival home after the Olympic Games, crowds thronged the 15-mile route from Piarco to Port-of-Spain to greet the new hero, and at the airport itself the Prime Minister and members of government turned up to offer an official welcome. Shortly afterwards, all sorts of honours were heaped upon him. Among these was the fact that an aircraft was named after him straightaway, and a few weeks later, at the nation's Independence Awards Ceremony, Hasely Crawford was given the nation's highest award, the Trinity Cross.

Because of his new-found prominence, not only those in the outside world but those in Trinidad to whom he was not known before would have liked to ask the question: Who is Hasely Crawford?

Hasely Crawford was born at number 19 Sutton Street in San Fernando on 16 August, 1950. His first school was San Fernando Boys Government, and while there as an infant of about 7, playing with other little boys of his own age, he realised that he could run. Naturally, this did not mean much to him at that stage. He briefly attended the Asja School, and later went to the San Fernando Technical School, where he had an outstanding career as a student. He was very good with his hands and had great aptitude for the technical life. He got through certain aspects of the curriculum before the normal time and in the final examination excelled in machine shop craft. He then went to Texaco as an apprentice and had the distinction of having 15 months deducted from his 5-year apprenticeship period, because of his performance at the Technical School. He started his career there in a special apprentice pilot scheme, as an apprentice bench-fitter.

But fortunately for us, settling down to life as a bench-fitter was not to be the course of Hasely's life. There were scores of bench-fitters, but few with the exceptional ability that sprint champions are made of. He was now 19, and in the space between childhood and adolescence he did not only take note of the fact that he could run, but had done exceptionally well, first at school sports and later at more elaborate athletic games. Now in 1969, he took up running seriously, and it was not long before he caught the attention of officials.

In early 1971, he was offered an athletic scholarship to the University of Eastern Michigan in the United States. Unhappily though, just at this juncture, he met with a serious traffic accident and could not compete for a year. He was in serious training after recovering from the accident and when he next competed, which was in May 1972, he opened up a new phase for himself, confirming that he was not just a good athlete but an international sprinter. On that date, among other runners at a sports meeting in Kentucky, he came second in a 100 yards event with a time of 9.4 seconds.

It is this time we have to consider. In 1947, McDonald Baily equalled the British record 3 times for the 100 yards: and that time was 9.7 seconds. The Trinidad record at that time was held by George Lewis at 9.8 seconds. Here was a young athlete returning 9.4 seconds in one of his first big sports meeting.

Hasely's rise was like a meteor, quick and dazzling. That very year, 1972, he was chosen to represent this country at the Olympic Games at Munich and after reaching the finals—in itself no mean feat—injury to his left eye spoiled his chances. He officially finished 8th.

It was the following Olympic Games which saw Hasely at the height of his powers. Hasely was chosen once again to represent Trinidad and Tobago at Montreal and of course the scene has already been described. Hasely dashed down the lanes to cover himself with glory.

CHAPTER FIFTYFIVE

THE FIRST WORLD CHAMPION (1981)

C heers rent the air as the referee raised the hand of the victor. The seconds in the red-white-and-black corner rushed into the ring. The victor was not in the least surprised about his victory, but for his seconds, it was a bewildering, incredible moment.

As the referee announced the decision, the victor thinks of home, which is thousands of miles across the seas, and he knew that there was a mass of jubilant people over there, thrilled to witness on television this historic event. It was very like a dream. The cheers still resounded and the gloved hand was still in the air. The boxer covered in glory was none other than Claude Noel, the new lightweight champion of the world. The date was 12 September, 1981, and it was the first time in history that a champion of the world came from Trinidad and Tobago.

In boxing circles everywhere, and indeed among all observers of the scene, the question was being asked: Why Trinidad and Tobago? What is responsible for this tiny republic commanding the attention of the world? For they recalled that Hasely Crawford became the Olympic 100-metre sprint champion in 1976; that Penny Commisiong won the "Miss Universe" title in 1977; that Jean Pierre and her net-ballers all but hit the top of the netball world in 1979. Why, Trinidad and Tobago, indeed! And who is Claude Noel?

Claude Noel was born at Roxborough, Tobago, on 25 July, 1948. His first school was the Roxborough Boys' E.C., but at the tender age of ten he was sent to live with an aunt in Trinidad. Shortly afterwards he was put into the orphan home at Belmont. Life for the boy became very tumultuous. Because of constant fighting with boys of his own age and older, during which he must have won many battles (unpaid), he was advised to see J.M. Douglas, who gave boxing lessons there at the time. Claude—maybe for once— did as he was told, because in fact there was a lot to inspire the youngster. The orphanage had many bright young boxing prospects, among them the noted Jimmy Duncan, and it was from the orphanage that former light heavyweight champion of Trinidad, Gentle Daniel, came. But before Claude could reflect on this properly, he was transferred from the Belmont orphanage to the St. Michael School for Boys, because he could not stop fighting.

At that time, he was only 13 and determined to get into the ring. At St. Michael's, he met Ken Matthias, the boxer, who was one of the officers at the school. Claude Noel joined the ranks of the amateurs, and with Ken's coaching, he became very much aware of his talent. However, fights were hard to come by (that is, the paid ones), and he, a featherweight, weighing 126 pounds, was forced to accept bouts with much heavier men. This would have been tough on the average boxer, but Claude Noel was no average boxer, and his fellow amateurs seemed so easily put away that he decided to turn professional after only eight amateur fights.

Noel's first professional fight was against Michael Baptiste, the welterweight, who was entering the ring at 147 pounds. Claude tried hard but could reach no more than 131 pounds and the regulations required him to make a minimum of 136. However, there is always a way to put on weight quickly if you have the right handler. His trainer judiciously tied a few pounds of lead around the waist of Claude Noel and he tipped the scales at 139. Baptiste was surprised that Claude had made the weight, but Claude was not a bit surprised. Anyway, he entered the ring with Baptiste and knocked him out in the fourth round.

Claude was not content. After just one fight, he was already looking at the championship, for he felt he was born to be king. At that time, the lightweight champion of Trinidad was Fitzroy Giuseppi, a fighter with no less than 50 battles to his name. Claude asked for a championship fight with Giuseppi, but Giuseppi's camp dismissed him, saying that he was not ready. As a concession, Giuseppi's manager told him that if he had one more fight he could re-apply. Claude signed up to fight Selwyn Figaro, and without lead he was able to reach 136 pounds as compared to Figaro's weight of 147 pounds. He stopped Figaro in the eighth round.

So now he was able to fight for the lightweight crown. He entered the ring very much the unfancied boxer but he upset all predictions by knocking out Giuseppi in the tenth round to win the Lightweight Boxing Championship of Trinidad and Tobago. The year was 1976.

However, 1977 proved an unlucky year for Claude Noel, for in that year he was stopped twice by Lennox Blackmoor of Guyana. In 1978, he came back strongly, disposing of Hector Medina, and finding himself ranked eighth in the world. A number of victories after this lifted him to the position of Number One contender for the lightweight championship, then vacated by Roberto Duran of Panama. He then fought with Ernesto España for the championship, but the Venezuelan stopped him in the 13th. Again he fought back in the rankings to be Number One contender. The World Boxing Authority barred him from a return with Espana, but after defeating them in court, Espana refused to meet him. The then champion, Sean O'Grady, was stripped of his title, and Claude Noel fought for the world crown against the Number Two contender, Rudolfo Gonzalez (El Gato) of Mexico.

The fight took place on 12 September, 1981, and, yes, it is this historic moment we are recording here—the moment when Trinidad and Tobago got a world champion for the first time.

SOURCES

Chapter 1
Documents of the third voyage of Christopher Columbus. (TTHS 127)
Columbus' description of his Third Voyage.
"Admiral of the Ocean Sea" by Samuel Eliot Morrison.

Chapter 2
Columbus' description of his Third Voyage. (Major and Morrison)
Account of the Expedition of Antonio Sedeno. (TTHS 166)
Trinidad and Tobago Historical Society, Paper 109.
Appointment of Antonio Sedeno as Governor of Trinidad.

Chapter 3
The founding of San José by Domingo de Vera. (TTHS 15)
Antonio de Berrio's letter to the King of Spain, Jan. 1, 1593. (TTHS 16)
Antonio de Berrio's letter to the King of Spain 24/11/1593. (TTHS 18)

Chapter 4
Woodford to Bathurst (Sec. of State) 8/2/1816.
The founding of San José by Domingo de Vera.
Report on the death of Governor José y Eschales, December 1699.
Report of the Arena Massacre.

Chapter 5
History of Tobago by Henry Iles Woodcock Tobago, by C.R. Ottley.
Documents on Tobago translated and published by the Trinidad and Tobago Historical Society.

Chapter 6
History of Tobago by Henry Iles Woodcock Tobago, by C.R. Ottley.
Documents on Tobago translated and published by the Trinidad and Tobago Historical Society.

Chapter 7 and 8
Documents on Tobago published and translated by the Trinidad and Tobago Historical Society.

Chapter 9
Visit of Roume de St. Laurent to Trinidad in 1777.
Roume de St. Laurent to the Court of Spain.
The Cedula of Population of 1783.

Chapter 10
History of Trinidad by L.M. Fraser (Ch. VII).
Capitulation agreement between Abercromby and Chacón of
18/2/1 797.

Chapter 11
Despatch from Chacón to Council of the Indies, Madrid, announcing the fall of Trinidad, 27/2/1797.
Report from Abercromby to Sectretary of State Dundas describing seizure of Trinidad, 27/2/1797.

Despatch from Admiral Harvey to Secretary of Admiralty, 21/2/1797.
Report and map of Captain Frederick Mallet to Abercromby, July, 1797.

Chapter 12
History of Trinidad by L.M. Fraser.
Plan of the town of Port-of-Spain after the fire of 1808.

Chapter 13
History of the Trinidad Police Force by C.R. Ottley.
History of Trinidad by L.M. Fraser.
Documents relating to early Port-of-Spain and published by the Trinidad and Tobago Historical Society.
Port-of-Spain Gazette, 1825-1850.

Chapter 14
Survey of old newspapers at the West Indian reference and in the National Archives.

Chapter 15
Port-of-Spain Gazette of March 1850.
Interviews with descendants of Jean-Michel Cazabon, Trinidad and Tobago Yearbook of 1889.
Albums on Cazabon's paintings "18 Views of Trinidad" in 1851, and album of 1865.

Chapter 16
History of Trinidad by L.M. Fraser.
Duplicate despatches; Governor Woodford to Bathurst (Sec. of State), 1816-1820.
Harris to Grey 1850-1851 (Colonial Office papers)

Chapter 17
Port-of-Spain Gazette, March 1836.
Centenary Publication of St. Joseph's Convent, 1936.
History of Trinidad by E.L. Joseph.
Research on founding of Catholic institutions.
"At Last, A Christmas in the West Indies," by Charles Kingsley.

Chapter 18
The Emancipation Act, August 28, 1833
Port-of-Spain Gazette, August 1833 to August 1834 (especially August 5, 1834).
Port-of-Spain Gazette, August to September 1838.
Capadose's report on Emancipation Day.

Chapter 19
Based on reports of the emancipation and the abolition of slavery.

Chapter 20
Port-of-Spain Gazette, September 17, 1844.

Chapter 21
Port-of-Spain Gazette, 30th May 1845.
List of passengers on Fatel Rozack.
Duplicate despatches from Governor Macleod to the Secretary of States 1840 to 1844.
Duplicate despatches from Lord Harris to Secretary of States 1846 to 1851.

Chapter 22

Ordinance 8 of 1849, the Division of the Island into Counties and Wards.

Chapter 23
Ordinance 2 of 1851, for the Establishment of a Public Library in the town of Port-of-Spain.
Royal Gazette, 7th February, 1851.
Port-of-Spain Gazette, February to June, 1851.

Chapter 24
Harris to Grey duplicate despatches, 1846.
Report and advertisements of Water Company in 1846.
Port-of-Spain Gazette, October 1850.
Harris to Secretary of States.
Duplicate Despatches of 1850.
Report of water works for 1851.
Water Ordinance No. 18 of November 1851.

Chapter 25
Ordinance of 1851.
Keenan Report of 1870.

Chapter 26
Port-of-Spain Gazette, March 5, 1859.
San Fernando Gazette, 1858-1880.
Trinidad and Tobago Year Book 1900-1930.

Chapter 28
Wall and Sawkins Report, 1860.
Port-of-Spain Gazette, 1867.
Charles Kingsley's "At Last."

Chapter 29
Port-of-Spain Gazette, August, 1846.
Port-of-Spain Gazette, September, 1873.
Port-of-Spain Gazette, August 31, 1876.
Guppy's Year Book for 1877.
Trinidad Blue Book for 1876-1877.
Port-of-Spain Gazette, September 2, 1876.

Chapter 30
Port-of-Spain Gazette, December 27, 1883.
Debates of the Legislative Council, 1883-1884.

Chapter 31
Port-of-Spain Gazette and New Era, January 1885.
New Era, December 30, 1884.
Debates of the Legislative Council, 1883, 1884, 1885.
Debates of the Port-of-Spain Borough Council, 1883, 1884, 1885.
Guppy's Yearbook, 1884, 1885, 1886.

Chapter 32
Report of Royal Commission on Franchise for 1888 and Evidence at Fifth Company Baptist Church, April 9, 1888.
Trinidad's later political development.

Chapter 33
Hansard 1880 - 1900.
Documents on Tobago published by the Trinidad and Tobago Historical Society.
History of Tobago by Henry Iles Woodcock.
History of Tobago by C.R. Ottley.
Official Report on the Belmanna Riots, 1876.
Tobago's House of Assembly report for 1876.
Royal Gazette for 1877.
Order-in-Council on Tobago (1889).

Chapter 34
Fraser's History of Trinidad.
Port-of-Spain Gazette, April 5, 1890.

Chapter 35
Hansard 1894 - 1895.
Port-of-Spain Gazette, March 4, 1895.
Collens' Year Book, 1896.

Chapter 36
Port-of-Spain Gazette, June 1895.
Debates in the Legislative Council, 1894 - 1896.
Collens' Year Book for 1896.

Chapter 37
Port-of-Spain Gazette March - April, 1900.
Collens' Year Book for 1900.

Chapter 38
Port-of-Spain Gazette, February, 1900.
Port-of-Spain Gazette, 1880 - 1900.

Chapter 39
Port-of-Spain Gazette, 1902.
Trinidad and Tobago Year Book, 1901.

Chapter 40
Interviews with relatives of Asgaralli Syne and Mrs. Charles.
Port-of-Spain Gazette, 1911-1913 and 1920-1935.
Franklin's Yearbook, 1912 - 1935.
Royal Gazette notice of 1912.

Chapter 41
Port-of-Spain Gazette, January-March, 1913.
Collens' Yearbook, 1914.
The Cinema World in Port-of-Spain from "The Making of Port-of-Spain."

Chapter 42
Port-of-Spain Gazette, January 24, 1913.
Collens' Yearbook, 1914.

Chapter 43
Port-of-Spain Gazette, December 23, 1919.

Cipriani's career from "The Making of Port-of-Spain".

Chapter 44
Port-of-Spain Gazette, February 8, 1925.

Chapter 45
Port-of-Spain Gazette, September 24, 1929.
Franklin's Yearbook of 1930.

Chapter 46
Career of Mikey Cipriani from "The Making of Port-of-Spain."
Port-of-Spain Gazette 2nd to 13th June 1934.

Chapter 47
Trinidad Guardian, January 18, 1935.
"The Making of Port-of-Spain."

Chapter 48
"Port-of-Spain gets a deep-water harbour" from "The Making of Port-of-Spain." Trinidad
Guardian, 1939.

Chapter 49
"Port-of-Spain in a World at War."

Chapter 50
"Port-of-Spain in a World at War".

Chapter 51
Trinidad Guardian, July 3, 1946.
Trinidad and Tobago Year Book for 1947.

Chapter 52
Trinidad Guardian, September 2, 1962.
Hansard 1962.
"Road to Independence," unpublished document on Trinidad's political progress.

Chapter 53
Trinidad Guardian, August - September 1962.
Debates January-August 1962.

Chapter 54
Interview with Hasely Crawford, Trinidad Guardian and Trinidad Express, July 24 1976.

Chapter 55
Trinidad Guardian and Trinidad Express reports for September 13, 1981.